WINE
UNCORKED

WINE
UNCORKED
FRED SIRIEIX

with Dan Hurst

*My guide to
the World
of Wine*

EBURY
SPOTLIGHT

1 3 5 7 9 10 8 6 4 2

Ebury Spotlight, an imprint of Ebury Publishing
20 Vauxhall Bridge Road
London SW1V 2SA

Ebury Spotlight is part of the Penguin Random House
group of companies whose addresses can be found at global.
penguinrandomhouse.com

Penguin
Random House
UK

Design by Nikki Ellis
Additional cover design by Clarkevanmeurs Design

First published by Ebury Spotlight in 2022

www.penguin.co.uk

A CIP catalogue record for this book is available
from the British Library

ISBN 9781529149555

Printed and bound in Great Britain by Clays Ltd,
Elcograf S.p.A. Imported into the EEA by Penguin
Random House Ireland, Morrison Chambers,
32 Nassau Street, Dublin D02 YH68.

MIX
Paper from
responsible sources
FSC
www.fsc.org   FSC® C018179

Penguin Random House is committed
to a sustainable future for our business,
our readers and our planet. This book is
made from Forest Stewardship Council®
certified paper.

To my children, Andrea and Matteo Lucien,
my publishers Lorna and Michelle
and my agent Grant.

Special thanks to Joelle and Erik.

Contents

Part 2: Wine Regions   **47**

Introduction

Wine was a part of my life long before I ever had my first sip. Like most people in France, my parents have never drunk a lot, but they do drink often, and growing up in Limoges, every lunch and dinner would be accompanied with a small glass of the wine *en vrac* (in bulk) that my father would buy from a local wine cellar every few weeks and decant into bottles himself at home. A bottle would be opened and set on the table at the beginning of the week and both my parents would enjoy a couple of fingers of it with every meal over the course of the next few days. It was never to excess, but it was always there.

This everyday wine was not what we served to guests. For that, my father would travel to Saint-Emilion every September and work in the vineyards, harvesting grapes. He would return, sun-kissed from working in the fields, and with the boot of his car loaded with the clinking bottles that he accepted as payment for his hard work. This wine would be reserved for special occasions, weekends and holidays, and every time he poured a glass for someone new, he would ask proudly, 'Can you taste my secateurs?'

And he was right to ask. Every glass of wine is brimming with memories; from the rich soil that nourishes the vine, to the warm sun that ripens the fruit, to the hand holding the secateurs that cuts the grapes. Everything that goes into growing and producing a particular vintage is right there if you know where to find it. For me, though, the most important memories are those that are made while enjoying the wine. A sip of an Alsatian *vendanges tardives*, a wine made with late-harvest grapes that have been allowed to hang on the vine to intensify their sugary sweetness, takes me straight back to family Christmases when my grandfather would serve it with a delicious terrine at the start of the meal – a sweet, syrupy nectar to cut through the richness of the food. Likewise, a glug of intensely fruity Beaujolais Nouveau, a wine that is bottled and on the shelves just a few weeks after the grapes are harvested, takes me back to my days at catering college, where my classmates and I marvelled at its intense fruitiness and merrily glugged bottle after delicious bottle. Oh là là.

In my childhood home, every meal was a ritual. Regardless of whether we had company or not, the table was always properly set and we would sit together for three courses each evening, catching up on the day and enjoying the delicious meal that my mother had conjured from the kitchen despite having been out at work all day. My family were not particularly wealthy – both my parents worked as nurses in a local hospital – but at the end of each day we ate like royalty.

At weekends or celebrations, my parents would entertain on a grander scale. I remember pits being dug in the garden and whole lambs being roasted over a live fire on giant spits. People would gather to enjoy the feast and share stories over wine late into the evening. It was here that I learnt the power of great food and wine to bring people together. Food and drink were at the centre of everything and we built a community of family and friends and many, many great memories around it.

By the time I was in my teens, I too was allowed a very small glass of wine with my meal on special occasions. It's telling that I don't remember the first time this happened in the same way that the first time I shared a beer with my father sticks in my memory – there was no fanfare or celebration, it was just a case that food and wine went hand in hand in that house. And for me they still do – I cannot rush through a meal or eat just for speed or convenience. I need the ritual.

It was this love for the theatre of dining that pulled me towards my career working front of house in restaurants. At age 16, I attended catering college with the intention of becoming a chef, but quickly I began to feel that it wasn't quite the right fit. In the kitchen, I felt constrained, like a factory worker on a production line. I longed to be out among the diners, soaking up the atmosphere. Working front of house can be a very hard job, but it is also a privilege to play a small part in the creation of these special memories, memories that are fuelled by delicious food and great wine.

Despite my decision not to be a chef, I owe a lot to the time I spent in the kitchen at catering college. Not only has it made me a better cook, but this grounding gave me a great understanding of flavour and technique. This was the mid 1980s and France was still very much the centre of the food and wine world – especially to those of us who lived there. So the focus was very much on French food and French wine. It was the same at home – my parents only ever drank wine from France. When I visit my father now, I like to take him a special bottle from elsewhere in the world – an earthy Italian Barolo, perhaps, or an intensely fruity Californian Cabernet – and he will drink and enjoy them, but he always returns to France. That is what he knows. But, for me, it was at catering college that I started to first understand how huge and complex the world of wine actually is. We would have wine tastings where we would learn about the different wine regions of France and all the special ways in which the climate and traditions of each region had an impact on what ended up in the glass, and I would marvel at how such seemingly small differences could have such a huge effect on the end result. Bolstered with this new knowledge, the appreciation for wine I learned in my parents' house quickly developed into a passion, and I have been hungry to keep trying new things ever since. As my life expanded, through travelling the world and working in wonderful restaurants, so too did my understanding of wine. I left France behind, both physically and metaphorically, and discovered the wonderful wines produced all around the world. I still love French wine, but run your finger down the bottles stored in my wine rack and you will travel the world.

When I first arrived in London, I took this love of wine a step further and decided to broaden my understanding by studying at the Wine & Spirit Education Trust. I was never interested in becoming a sommelier, but I was fascinated by wine and was often asked to recommend wines in the restaurants that I worked in, so I wanted to learn as much as possible.

Understanding wine is like understanding music: there are always new discoveries to be made. In music there are so many genres, and within each of these genres there are thousands of different branches that each take you in a different direction. Wine is the same. As an example, you may think you like Sauvignon Blanc, but two bottles made with the same grape can taste completely different. A French Sauvignon Blanc, where the grapes are grown in a cooler climate and spend longer on the vine, has a grassy mineral taste, whereas grapes grown in the warmer climes of Australia or New Zealand, where the grapes ripen faster, can be more fruity and tropical. Armed with this knowledge you might decide

that what you like is a French Sauvignon Blanc, but if you mined down even further you may find that the Sauvignon Blanc from Bordeaux is too fruity for your taste, in which case you may want to look north, to the Loire Valley, where the flinty soil imparts a crisper, more mineral taste. And here, again, you are faced with more questions. As you look down the wine list you see only wines from the Loire listed as Sancerre or Pouilly-Fumé, but though you might struggle to find it on the label, did you know that these were in fact made with Sauvignon Blanc grapes? Beyond that, you get into individual producers and winemaking techniques, whether the wine is aged in oak and, if so, for how long, or even what the weather was like on a particular year. There are always further layers.

The good news is that I have no interest in making you a Master of Wine – this is not that book. In fact, there is no book in existence that could do that. Training to the highest levels of wine appreciation takes years of study and there are only a very small handful of people in the world who have reached those heights. Full disclosure: I am not one of them. Who I am is someone who loves wine and knows enough about it to make confident

choices that mostly pay off. And that's what this book is about: choices. I can't tell you which bottles of wine you will love – our tastes may be completely different – but I can give you the knowledge and information that YOU need to help YOU identify what YOU are looking for in a glass of wine.

Though I love wine, there is a snobbery around it that I can't stand. Over the centuries a mythology has built up that can feel impossible to navigate – there are rules. Perhaps it's because I'm French, but I've never been much of a rule follower, so while I will lay them out in this book, I will also tell you why they don't matter. After all, it's only a drink. And in life we can and should do whatever we like!

Fred

PART ONE

The Basics

How wine is made

To understand what's in your bottle, it helps to have an understanding of how it got there. Different wine-making regions around the world have their own laws around how wine is produced and subsequent classification and gradings on the finished product. This is especially true in Old World countries such as France (Appellation d'Origine Contrôlée/AOC) and Italy (Denominazione di Origine Controllata e Garantita/DOCG), which are both governed by strict regulations that control everything, from which grapes can be used in a specific region, the alcohol content of the wine, how often grapes are watered and the age of the vines themselves. Because of this there is no one defined set of 'rules' for how wine is made, but there are some key stages that are present in the making of every bottle. The process outlined below is a general overview of how most red, white and sparkling wines are made.

1. The grapes are harvested

Once ripe, the grapes are picked from the vines, either by hand or by using mechanical grape harvesters. This usually happens in the autumn, when the grapes are beautifully ripe, but before the temperature drops to a point that could damage the grapes. White grapes are picked slightly earlier than red to retain some of their acidity. For dessert wine, the grapes are left on the vine for longer to dry out and intensify their sweetness – this process is called 'raisinating'.

2. The grapes are crushed
(and most of the time pressed)

This process is slightly different for red and white wines. With red wines, the grapes are crushed, and any bits of stem or stray leaves are removed, but the skins are retained. It is important to realize that regardless of the colour of a wine, all grape juice is white. It is the skin that gives red wine its deep ruby colour. (This explains why you often find red grapes used in white wines – Pinot Noir in Champagne, for example.) For white wine, the grapes are pressed to remove the skin and seeds at this stage, leaving just the juice. Rosé wine, which is made with red grapes, also retains the grape skins at this stage, but the skins are macerated with the juice for just a few hours to impart the soft blush colour that we associate with rosé wine, and are then pressed before fermentation.

3. The juice is fermented

The grape juice is transferred to large stainless steel fermentation tanks or wood barrels and yeast is added. Some winemakers only use natural yeasts, others use commercially produced varieties. Over the fermentation process the yeast reacts with the natural sugars in the grape juice and converts it into alcohol. A typical fermentation is usually around two weeks, though this can differ depending on the type of wine being produced.

For Champagne and sparkling wines that contain a blend of red and white grape juice, the juices are fermented separately and then blended to make a *cuvée*.

4. The wine is pressed and filtered

It is at this stage that red wine is pressed to remove the grape skin and seeds. White wines are filtered to remove any impurities.

5. The wine is bottled or aged (unless it's sparkling!)

Now the wine is either transferred to oak casks or stainless steel vats to settle and develop flavour, or bottled straight away. Wine stored in oak is typically aged for six to nine months, but this can be significantly longer or shorter depending on the wine that is being made. Still wines are then bottled and corked.

6. Champagne and sparkling wine is fermented for a second time

For Champagne and sparkling wine, the blend (*cuvée*) is transferred to bottles, fed with a little more yeast and sugar, and sealed tight with caps similar to those found on beer bottles. The wine now undergoes a second fermentation process, which is what gives it its signature bubbles. For Champagne, this process takes at least 18 months and up to several years, but for some sparkling wines it is much quicker. In the *méthode traditionnelle* – which is used in the production of Champagne and other sparkling wines such as Cava and Franciacorta – after fermentation the bottles are gradually tilted neck down and rotated in small increments over time, either mechanically or by hand, to move the sediment (lees) into the neck of the bottle. The liquid in the neck of the bottle is then frozen and the cap removed, so that the gas in the bottle pushes up the frozen sediment for easy removal. The wine is then corked and covered with a wire cage (a *muselet*) to keep the cork safely in place.

How to read a wine label

The biggest clue to knowing what's inside your bottle before you take the first sip is what's written on the label, so knowing how to navigate your way around one is crucial for anyone who is looking to expand their wine knowledge. The problem is, it's not that simple.

One of the reasons that wine can be so confusing is that there is no universal set of rules mandating what wine sellers need to tell you on the label. Buy almost any other packaged item of food or drink and you will find a full list of ingredients on the packet, but wine makes you work a bit harder. Depending on where the bottle is from, the label will give you different information and, with some wines, it definitely helps to have a little bit of knowledge to help you bridge the gaps. In France, for example, wines are labelled by region and not grape varietal, so you need to know which grapes are grown in which regions to work out what's actually in your glass. (To help with this, you'll find a list of key regions and their grape varietals in the introduction for each country in the second half of this book.) Wines produced in countries with younger winemaking traditions tend to have slightly more helpful labels, giving you both the grape varietal as well as the region where the wine is produced.

There are three main styles of wine label, though within each of these the information may vary from country to country, or even region to region. For this reason, the first thing to identify when looking at any bottle of wine is the country of origin. The following illustrations are examples of each of the three main types of wine label and show the information that you can expect to find on each. Pair this information with the guidance on regions in the second half of this book and you should have a good idea of what's in your bottle before you reach for the corkscrew.

1. By region

Countries that follow a strict appellation system, such as France, Italy, Spain and Portugal, label their wines by region or 'appellation' (roughly translated, 'appellation' means 'name' or 'designation'). An appellation is a legally defined geographical area that dictates which grapes can be grown within that area. Because of this, the grape or varietal is rarely marked on the bottle and the onus is on the drinker to know which grapes are grown in which region. The most widely recognised example of this is possibly Champagne, where only wines grown within the Champagne region can be labelled as such. The grapes used in Champagne are generally made up of a blend of Chardonnay, Pinot Noir and Pinot Meunier grapes, though you will never see this on the label. The importance of geographical provenance is further heightened in some regions by more specific grading classifications, for example France's *cru* system. To carry on the Champagne example, wines produced in just 17 villages in the region are granted *Grand Cru* status, the highest classification, which amounts to less than 10 per cent of all grapes grown in the region.

2. By varietal

Wines that aren't bound by strict appellation systems tend to be from the younger winemaking countries, often described as the 'New World' and covering the wines of the USA, Australia, New Zealand, South Africa and South America. Because there are no rules dictating which grapes can be grown in each region, these bottles are labelled by grape variety, so the labels tend to be a little easier to navigate. Depending on the country of origin there are different regulations around how much of the bottle's contents should be made up of the grape on the label – wines from the USA need to be made of at least 75 per cent of the labelled grape, for example, but the remaining 25 per cent can be a blend of any other type of grape. The more information a bottle with this type of label gives, the more chance you have of procuring a good-quality wine. Great winemakers like to get specific about the region that their grapes are grown in – they're rightly proud of what they produce and know that wine aficionados will be interested in the climate, landscape and techniques that go into making their wine. For example, a wine labelled 'produce of California' or 'South Australia' is less likely to be great than one that drills down into a specific area like, say, 'Napa Valley' or 'Barossa Valley'.

3. By name

Wines with pithy, made-up names on eye-catching labels can be some of the hardest to decipher as the names themselves tell you little about what's in the bottle, though look on the back of the bottle and you'll generally find a little more information. There are many reasons that a winery might decide on a made-up name rather than one of the labelling systems outlined above, but the most obvious is that it's clever marketing, designed to catch your eye. A great example of this style of marketing-led labelling is Whispering Angel, a Provençal rosé that has become increasingly popular in recent years. It is a delicious wine, perfect for quaffing on a summer's afternoon, but it is the clever name, luxury positioning and labelling that make it stand out from the raft of other similar wines on the market.

There are other reasons that a winery might decide to go down this route, with some winemakers looking to break free from the constraints of a tightly governed set of wine rules. The appellation systems of 'Old World' countries are designed to guarantee quality and tradition in the wines produced in their regions, but this leaves little room for those looking to experiment and challenge the boundaries of what's been done before – the punks of the wine world! A good example of this are the Sassicaia wines produced by Tenuta San Guido in Tuscany. These 'Super Tuscans' are regarded today as some of the world's finest wines, but when they were first released in 1966, the Italian classification system meant that they had to be labelled as 'vino da tavola' or table wine – Italy's lowest-ranking wine classification. The reason for this is that the winemakers had decided to buck with tradition and plant non-native Cabernet Sauvignon and Cabernet Franc grapes to produce their wines, thus breaking the rules of Italian winemaking, meaning that they could not follow the traditional Italian labelling system of leading by region. This lowly classification did little to hinder the reputation of the wine and, 10 years later, Sassicaia was named the world's best Cabernet at an international wine tasting in London. In the early 1990s, Sassicaia wines were finally granted their own appellation and are the only Italian wine from a single estate to have been granted the honour, but they had to break a few rules to get there.

Other information found on a wine label

Other information that can be found on a label can include the wine classification or grading depending on the country where it is produced (see the introduction to each of the countries covered in the second half of this book for more information about the wine classifications of different regions), the ABV (alcohol by volume)/alcohol percentage, the name of the producer or vineyard, where the wine was bottled and the vintage (year the grapes were picked).

An example of a wine that is labelled by grape varietal

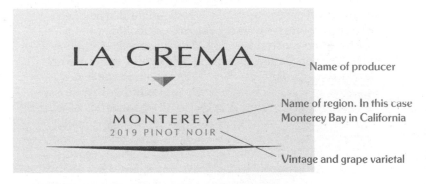

LA CREMA —— Name of producer

MONTEREY —— Name of region. In this case Monterey Bay in California

2019 PINOT NOIR —— Vintage and grape varietal

LA CREMA

PINOT NOIR
MONTEREY

CONTAINS SULFITES - VINTED AND BOTTLED BY LA CREMA, SANTA ROSA, CALIFORNIA
750ML - 13.5% ALC/VOL - 1.800.314.1762

GOVERNMENT WARNING: (1) ACCORDING TO THE SURGEON GENERAL, WOMEN SHOULD NOT DRINK ALCOHOLIC BEVERAGES DURING PREGNANCY BECAUSE OF THE RISK OF BIRTH DEFECTS (2) CONSUMPTION OF ALCOHOLIC BEVERAGES IMPAIRS YOUR ABILITY TO DRIVE A CAR OR OPERATE MACHINERY, AND MAY CAUSE HEALTH PROBLEMS.

Alcohol content (ABV) given on back label

An example of a wine that is labelled by region

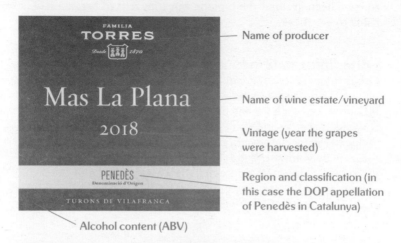

— Name of producer

— Name of wine estate/vineyard

— Vintage (year the grapes were harvested)

— Region and classification (in this case the DOP appellation of Penedès in Catalunya)

Alcohol content (ABV)

In this example an indication of grape varietal is only given on the back label, but often wines that are labelled in this way will not give this information at all

An example of a wine that is labelled by name

Wine name (in this case Sagre de Toro, translating to 'blood of the bull')

Vintage (year the grapes were harvested)

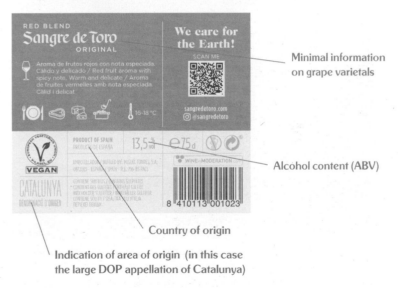

Minimal information on grape varietals

Alcohol content (ABV)

Country of origin

Indication of area of origin (in this case the large DOP appellation of Catalunya)

How to order wine in a restaurant

Being handed the wine list in a restaurant can feel like a huge responsibility. Not only do you want to pick a wine that everyone at the table will enjoy, but also one that complements the various meals that have been ordered and fits with everyone's budget. The best thing you can do is try to relax and enjoy the experience.

Cost is key _____ ££

On restaurant wine lists, mark-ups can typically range from 100 to 300 per cent of the retail price, though this can be significantly higher if you're ordering from the more exclusive end of the menu. If you're paying the bill yourself, then the world is your oyster in terms of what you want to pay, but if you're going to be splitting the bill then it is always a good idea to gauge how much everyone is happy to pay before making a selection. Once you've established the price bracket that you're comfortable within, you should have a much narrower selection of wines to choose from. Simply work out what your top level is and don't consider anything above it. Easy!

Ask the waiter _____ ££££

If you are lucky enough to be dining in a restaurant that has a wine waiter or sommelier and you are unsure which wine to order, then the best thing you can do is ask for their advice. Far from making you look like you don't know what you're doing, engaging them in this way shows that you have a passion for wine and want to order a great bottle – nothing wrong with that. The wine waiter knows the menus at their restaurant like the back of their hand, so should be really well placed to select a bottle that will appeal to you and match well with the food that you've selected. When it comes to price, the most elegant way of signifying how much you want to pay is to point to a similarly priced bottle on the list and say 'I'd like something around this price.'

When talking to a sommelier, the more information that you can give them the better. If you've recently loved a bottle of wine and want to find something similar then let them know. Giving them a solid reference point is a great way to help them home in on a wine that will suit your tastes. If you don't have any specific examples, tell them what you're looking for in a wine – red or white, dry or sweet, light or heavy, fruit-forward or more neutral, oaked or unoaked, whether you like something with heightened acidity or a touch of minerality coming through (more on those tasting notes on page 33). Another great way to engage the sommelier is to ask them what wine on their list they are the most excited about at the moment, or what they would order in the same price bracket. It's their job to help you find a great bottle of wine to go with your meal and they will be very grateful for you letting them do it.

Use your know-how_____£

If there isn't a wine waiter on hand, then use your own knowledge to narrow the field and select a bottle of wine that you will enjoy. If in doubt, play it safe and go for a variety that you know you'll appreciate. Because of restaurant mark-ups, making a mistake in a restaurant can be much costlier than when buying wine from a shop, so it makes sense to avoid anything that you really don't recognise. Most wine lists will give you the grape varietal, vintage, country, region of origin and even the individual vineyard name, so you should be able to piece together all of this information to land on something that you'll love. Why not keep this book tucked into the inside pocket of your jacket or your bag, if you're carrying one, and refer to it if you need a bit more guidance about anything that's on the wine list.

Food, glorious food_____£££

Generally, I don't really believe in worrying about pairing food with what you're drinking. Life's too short. Just drink and eat what you feel like in that moment, and you'll be sure to enjoy it. Red wine with fish? Go for it! Fancy a zesty white with a steak? Why not? This can be even more true in a restaurant situation, where there can be a whole host of different meals on the table at any one time. This said, I do like to make sure that the wine doesn't overpower the food and vice versa, so that red wine I'm going to enjoy with my fish might be something nice and light, like a Pinot Noir, rather than something too full-bodied that might kill the delicate flavours of my meal. Likewise, my steak needs a white wine that's robust enough to stand up to the richness of meat, so something like an oaky Chardonnay would be at the top of my list. (For more on pairing wine with food, see page 36.)

If in doubt, go for bubbles_____£££

Choosing a bottle of wine for a whole table of people all eating different meals can feel like an impossible task. Maybe someone is eating something rich and meaty, another something spicy and a third a light fish dish – how are you going to find something that will complement everyone's food? My top tip, when in doubt, order bubbles! Yes, it can be expensive to order Champagne in restaurants, but a nice Crémant, Cava or Prosecco will do just as well if you don't want to splurge, and with a glass of bubbles frothing in your hand it immediately feels like a celebration. Fizz is also a great option for when you first sit down and haven't had a chance to peruse the menu yet. Those bubbles will lift everyone's spirits and ensure you're in for a wonderful evening.

How to buy wine in a shop (or online)

Whether you're visiting a specialist wine shop or are just grabbing a couple of bottles in the local supermarket on your weekly food shop, it can be hard to know where to start when faced with never-ending shelves of seemingly identical bottles. The good news is that, compared to ordering wine in a restaurant, the pressure is off. So, use some of the advice below and try to enjoy the process.

Take your time

In a shop, where you don't have a waiter standing over you waiting to take an order (and a tableful of thirsty diners waiting for a glass of wine), you have the luxury of being able to spend a little more time making a decision. You can use the information in this book to find a bottle that you think you'll like, but there are also a host of great wine apps that will show you reviews of specific vintages, if you want to check the consensus on a particular bottle before committing to buying.

Be adventurous

For me, shopping for wine is like being a kid in a candy store – there's always something new that looks interesting. If I am buying a few bottles, I always like to get at least one that I've never tried before. It makes sense to be drawn to what you know and like, but the only way to expand your horizons is to try new things. The risk of getting something you don't enjoy is always there, but the financial risk is significantly lower than when you're ordering in a restaurant, and you can always use it for cooking if you make a choice that you're really not sure about. For example, maybe you know that you really love a Beaujolais, and because of that you're naturally drawn to wines that are light and fruity with low tannins and lovely acidity – you could either look for another wine that has a similar profile, a beautifully light Pinot Noir perhaps, or decide to get out of your comfort zone and try something bolder and more robust, but still with some of those lovely, smooth characteristics that you like, say a silky Spanish Rioja.

Shop big, shop small

Nowadays many supermarkets have wonderful wine selections that have been put together by a passionate and wonderfully trained staff of wine experts. Supermarkets have greater spending power, so they are able to sell wine at a slightly lower price than specialist wine stores. That said, if you're looking for something very specific or from a single producer, then it's best to do some research, go to a specialist supplier, and talk to them about your needs. In a wine shop you generally have the advantage of having some really knowledgeable and passionate staff on hand who will love nothing more than having a chat with you about your wine needs (and may even give you a cheeky taste, if they're feeling generous!).

Spend what you can afford

I have had great bottles of wine that have cost hundreds of pounds and I have had (many more) great wines that cost a fraction of that price. If you have deep pockets then by all means use them, but there is still plenty of fun to be had for the wine buyer on a leaner budget. A great example of how to do this is with Champagne. We all know Champagne can be expensive. It is built on a reputation of luxury and exclusivity that only adds to the thrill of popping that cork. But if you look away from the big houses then there are wonderful examples to be found at more competitive prices. 'Grower' Champagne is exactly what the name implies – Champagne made by the growers. Typically, large Champagne houses will buy their

grapes from lots of different growers and mix grapes from different regions into a *cuvée* that is unique to them. For these high-end producers consistency is key, and what they put out must taste the same each year. Grower champagne is different in that it is made by the people who own the vineyards themselves, so is much more reflective of their specific *terroir* (the landscape the grapes are grown in, the richness of the soil, the climate that particular year), and as such the taste can change year on year. In some ways it's a more artisan product, rather than the heavily controlled production of the large Champagne houses where the aim is uniformity. In grower wines you can taste the subtle changes depending on the vintage, and they can be very special as a result. It's worth noting that you might not find grower Champagnes in your local supermarket, but some specialist stores do stock them and they are widely available online.

Buying wine online

Shopping for wine on the internet comes with several advantages – you can search for more information about a specific wine, read customer or professional reviews and research the best producers and vintages, taking a lot of the guesswork out of your purchase. Once you know what wine you want to buy, you can also shop around for the best price. Plus, the sheer volume of wines online will vastly eclipse anything you would find in a shop. Shipping can be expensive, but buying a few bottles or even a whole crate of wine in a single purchase can help with this. Many online retailers will offer a reduced price if you buy several bottles of wine, so it's worth looking around for the best deals.

How to store wine

There is a commonly held belief that wine improves with age, which for the most part simply isn't true – most wines are best drunk within a year or two of purchase, especially if stored at room temperature. So where does this idea come from? We've all seen images of dusty wine cellars laden with bottle after bottle of precious wine, and there is a romantic notion of laying down a special bottle for just the right occasion – a wedding, an anniversary, the birth of a child. I don't hold with this. Wine is made to be enjoyed and laying a bottle down for a day that may never come is the opposite of enjoyment. By all means, celebrate those special occasions with a wonderful wine, but there's no need to sit on it for years beforehand.

That said, I would be lying if I said that a small percentage of wines didn't benefit from being laid down for a few years before opening, but these are far rarer than those that are ready to drink straight from the shop. Surely, far worse than drinking a wine too early, a bigger crime would be to open a beautiful bottle to find that it has lost its vibrancy and flavour, or worse, turned to vinegar?

If you are planning on keeping wine for an extended period, it's best to look to rich, full-bodied, tannic reds, which will open up and reveal more complexity through the aging process. Good examples of wines that respond well to being stored for a few years are high-end Bordeaux and Barolos. Never try and keep anything with a screwcap for a long time – these bottles are airtight, and the wine won't develop in the same way as wine stopped with a cork (where a very small amount of air can permeate) will. If you are going to cellar your wine, use the guidelines on the next page to ensure that you are keeping it in the best environment.

Keep it dark

As well as affecting the temperature of the wine adversely, exposing wine to sunlight can actually change it on a molecular level – and not in a good way! Wine that is exposed to UV rays from the sun (or fluorescent light), even for only a short time, can start to become pungent and its taste may be spoiled, due to the UV reacting with the naturally occurring riboflavin (vitamin B) to create sulphur compounds. White wine is more susceptible to this, but any bottle will be affected over time, so be sure to store your wine somewhere nice and dark.

Keep it calm

When storing wine, it is best to keep the bottles in a place where they won't be disturbed – definitely not on top of the washing machine! Even small vibrations can disturb the sediment in a bottle and prevent it from aging favourably.

Keep it cool

Wine needs to be stored at a consistent, cool temperature (ideally 12–15°C). If you are lucky enough to have a cellar then do make use of it, but a wine cooler/fridge also works well. (A wine fridge should be set at around 12–15°C for reds and 7–11°C for whites.) Humidity is also a factor (the ideal being 60–68 per cent), as storing wine at low humidity can cause the corks to dry out, exposing the wine to oxygen.

Keep it horizontal

Keeping the cork moist is why wine typically is stored horizontally. Again, this prevents the cork from drying out and leaving the wine vulnerable to damage from exposure to oxygen.

How to serve wine

We all know how to pour a glass of wine, but are we getting the best out of what's in the bottle? The wine rules that we have all had drummed into us time and again stipulate that red wine should be served at room temperature and white wine from the fridge, but the world has changed dramatically since these rules were made. Modern homes are heated to a much higher temperature than they once were; so hot in fact that the 'room temperature' you are serving your expensive bottle of red at could actually be damaging your wine. For red wines, chilling to between 14 and 16°C (57–61°F) is ideal, knowing the wine in the glass will always warm up at room temperature. Anything over 20°C (68°F) can diminish flavour and freshness and bring a harsh alcohol tang to the fore, especially if the bottle has sat in your house at that temperature for a couple of weeks before opening.

As a general rule for both reds and whites, the more full-bodied a wine is, the higher the temperature it should be served. Heavily chilling a full-bodied white will dampen its bouquet and dull its flavour, so it will need only a little time in the fridge to bring it down to an ideal temperature. Lighter-bodied whites, such as Pinot Grigio, Picpoul de Pinet or unoaked Chardonnay, benefit from longer chilling (a couple of hours in the fridge is fine) to heighten acidity and unlock delicate aromas.

With red wines, the richer, more full-bodied varieties are at their best just below room temperature, so may benefit from 10 minutes or so in the fridge before serving. Lighter reds, such as Pinot Noir or Beaujolais, benefit from a little more chilling, the idea being to serve them when they are just cool, rather than cold. To achieve this, rather than keeping them in the fridge long-term, a good idea is to transfer to the fridge for around an hour before serving.

Champagne and sparkling varieties need the most chilling – the ideal temperature being between 8 and 10°C. The simple reason for this is that, when it comes to bubbles, warm equals flat. Once the cork on a bottle of Champagne or sparkling wine is popped, the CO_2 that gives the wine its signature fizz starts to escape rapidly. Cold wine stays fizzier for longer as the CO_2 dissolves more easily in cooler temperatures. The warmer the wine is, the less soluble the CO_2 is and the more quickly it escapes. At Christmas, when the Champagne is flowing and the weather in my part of the world tends to be chilly, I like to keep a few bottles of Champagne outside to grab as needed and use nature's fridge to keep it at the perfect temperature.

To decant or not to decant

A decanter of wine on a dinner table can look very elegant and add a hint of sophistication to an occasion, but is it strictly necessary to decant or even 'breathe' your wine before serving?

There are two reasons why you may want to decant a wine. The first is to remove any sediment from the bottle. Sediment is a harmless by-product of fermentation and is generally only found in wines that have been in the bottle for at least 10 years, and is far more common in reds than whites, so this is only a factor to consider for older red wines. If you've been storing your wine horizontally, it's a good idea to stand it upright for at least 24 hours to let any sediment sink to the bottom of the bottle before decanting. When you're ready to decant, open the bottle, remove the foil and very slowly pour the wine into the decanter so that it runs down the inside edge of the glass and is distributed as widely as possible (this will help oxygenate

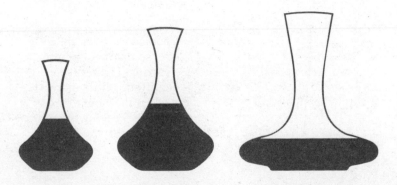

the wine, *see below*). Hold the bottle up to the light occasionally to check how clear the remaining wine in the bottle is, and once the sediment reaches the neck of the bottle, stop decanting immediately. Because wines that are being decanted for sediment tend to be at least 10 years old (some can be younger), it's important not to decant them too early before drinking, as prolonged exposure to air can actually damage particularly old or fragile wines. For older wines, a good rule of thumb is to decant the wine just before your guests arrive or a maximum of a couple of hours before drinking.

The second reason that you might decant a wine is to introduce some air and let the wine breathe. For younger wines that haven't had a chance to fully develop, decanting and letting them sit for a couple of hours can emulate the aging process and open up the flavour of the wine. This is particularly true for full-bodied tannic reds that would otherwise benefit from being aged for a few years in the bottle. The best way to test whether your wine would benefit from decanting is to open the bottle ahead of time and give it a sniff and a taste. If it doesn't smell of much, or seems 'closed', it may benefit from being decanted a couple of hours before serving. Decanting, in this case, will develop and open up the flavour and mellow and balance the wine.

A note on decanters
Though a decanter can look lovely on a table, don't worry if you don't have one. Wine can just as easily be decanted into a jug and then siphoned back into the bottle just before serving. If you don't have a decanter and do want to buy one, look for one with a long neck and a wide base, as this will provide maximum aeration for the wine. Glass or crystal is best as it allows you to see the colour of the wine and, crucially, how much is left.

Put a cork in it!

There is a belief that wines stoppered with cork are in some way superior to those sealed with screwcaps, but that simply isn't true. Cork is a brilliant option for wines that benefit from long storage and maturation as the naturally occurring air found inside the cork itself is emitted into the neck of the bottle as it is squeezed inside, thus allowing the wine to develop as it ages. Cork is also brilliantly sustainable – it is made from the bark of the cork oak and, crucially, can be harvested without felling the tree, meaning that over time the bark will grow back and cork can be cut from the same tree again and again. But cork also comes with problems. When we say a wine is 'corked', this refers to the presence of the chemical compounds 2,4,6-Trichloroanisole (TCA) or 2,4,6-Tribromoanisole (TBA), which react with wine to give it an unpleasant musty flavour and aroma. These compounds are a by-product of wood production and are transferred to wine directly by the cork. Corked wine happens more often than you might think (affecting around 7 per cent of cork-stopped wine).

Its occurrence can be very expensive and disappointing for the consumer and damaging for the reputation of the winery. For this reason, wines that are meant to be drunk young are now often sealed with metal screwcaps. Screwcaps don't emit air in the same way as cork, but for most white wines and lighter-bodied, fruity reds, this is preferable and means that the wine is as fresh and zesty the day it is poured as the day it first went into the bottle.

Like much of the snobbery in the world of wine, the belief that cork is somehow better stems from an unquestioning respect for tradition. It is the way it has always been done, therefore it must be the best way. As proof of this, in France, where tradition in winemaking is sacred, you will rarely find a bottle of wine that is sealed with a screwcap – it is widely believed to be the mark of an inferior wine. But if you move to the New World – for example, New Zealand – where winemaking isn't so entrenched in tradition and there is a willingness to experiment and move forward, 70 per cent of wine is sealed with a screwcap. I'm of the firm belief that both have their benefits and that neither is an indicator of quality, or lack thereof. Whichever side of the argument you fall on, there's no doubting that a screwcap makes it easier to get at the wine, and sometimes that's the most important thing of all.

The right glass for the job

As much as we might like to, we don't all have room in our homes for a set of special glasses for every type of wine. Part of the pleasure of going out for a fancy meal is the ceremony involved with the perfect piece of cutlery for every course and the right glass for every drink, but that's not how we live at home – it wouldn't be special otherwise. For me, in terms of the hierarchy of the wine, the company and the occasion, what I'm actually drinking out of comes fairly low down the list.

Some of my most memorable and enjoyable wines have been drunk out of paper cups at the beach or in the park, or, in my youth, even swigged straight from the bottle in the

welcome shade of a tree on a blistering hot day – so don't feel that you have to run out and buy an array of specialist glasses to truly enjoy wine. That said, a lovely glass can add a sense of occasion and elegance and make a nice bottle of wine that little bit more special. So what glasses should you invest in to enjoy wine at home?

Champagne and sparkling wine

For most people, Champagne or sparkling wine is saved for celebrations, and having the proper glass can add to the festivities. The two main types of glass for fizz are the flute and the coupe or saucer. Champagne flutes have tall, narrow bowls that taper in towards the mouth (for the purpose of reducing the surface area of the liquid in the glass and retaining as much fizz as possible) and long, thin stems. By contrast, the Champagne coupe or saucer has a wide, shallow bowl which, spurious legend has it, was modelled on the breast of Marie Antoinette. Personally, I like to drink Champagne out of a coupe because not only does the wine taste better, but it is also more fun – and that's what Champagne is all about! There are those who would argue that a flute keeps your fizz fizzier for longer – mine has never been around long enough to find out.

Red wine

The reason that red wine glasses are larger than white is to create maximum surface area, allowing the wine to breathe in the glass and ensuring that every time you take a sip all of the lovely aromas whoosh up your nose, enhancing the flavour of the wine. If you have deep pockets and lots of space in your cupboards, there are different glasses available for different styles of red wine. Glasses designed for Bordeaux have taller bowls to enable drinkers to swirl and aerate the wine, making them a great choice for full-bodied, tannic wines that need a bit of opening up before drinking. Burgundy glasses have larger, broader bowls to maximise the surface area and release the delicate aromas of lighter, full-bodied wines such as a Pinot Noir. They are also designed to deliver the wine straight to the sensitive tip of your tongue, making it easier to detect subtle nuances in the wine. These types of specialist wine glasses can make a very small difference to the wine on your palate, but for most people a single style of red wine glass is more than up to the job. Look for a variety with a large bowl and a tall stem. For a more intimate experience that allows you to feel closer to the wine as you swirl it in the bowl and pass it to your lips, opt for a delicate glass with as fine a rim as possible. Glasses with thicker rims tend to be heavy and inelegant, and can deaden the experience of tasting the wine.

White and rosé wine

White wine glasses generally have smaller, narrower bowls and slightly shorter stems than their red counterparts. The aromas in white wine are often more subtle, so the smaller bowl means that the wine is closer to your nose to detect the subtle bouquet in the glass and also limits the exposure of the wine to air, preserving the delicate flavours of the wine. The smaller bowl and shorter pour also aids with keeping white wine cool, something that isn't so much of a factor with red wines. As with red wine glasses, there are different styles of glass available for different styles of white wine. Wines with soft aromas, such as Sauvignon Blanc, Riesling or delicate rosés are suited to a narrow bowl that tapers in towards the mouth. This style traps the aroma of the wine in the glass and maximises the sensory experience of tasting the wine. Fuller-bodied, more pungent whites, such as oaky Chardonnays, benefit from a broader bowl and more interaction with the air. Chardonnay glasses have rounder bowls, similar to a red Burgundy glass, though are smaller in capacity. As with red wine glasses, a single style of glass is more than adequate unless you really want to push the boat out.

How to taste wine (and look like you know what you're doing)

In my parents' house, going out for dinner was a serious business. They would save up to visit the best restaurants and loved the sense of occasion and ceremony involved with fine dining, something that has definitely been passed on to me and reflected in my own choice of career. I remember vividly on one such occasion that the waiter brought a bottle of wine to the table and I found the way my father swirled it around the glass, held it up to the light and then stuck his nose in to give it a great sniff very, very funny. The following performance of sucking the wine through his teeth and swilling it around his mouth didn't help matters, and soon I was doubled over with laughter. The thing about tasting wine is that it *is* a bit of a performance, and one that I now undertake with relish. The key is not to be embarrassed – there is a reason for all these stages and your appreciation and understanding of wine will improve as a result.

1. Look
When presented with a glass of wine, the first thing to do is use your eyes. Hold it up to examine the colour of the wine and tilt the glass so that the light passes through it and you can appreciate how clear it is. As you become more familiar with different wines, you'll get a sense of what's in the glass from the colour alone. For white wines, richer, warmer colours indicate age and the possibility that the wine has been aged in oak, whereas younger wines tend to be paler. The opposite is true of reds, which tend to become paler as they age. With red wines, as well as colour, another thing to look for is

opacity – how easily light travels through the wine. This is a good indicator of body and structure. Wines that are more transparent tend to be lighter, whereas denser wines are heavier and fuller-bodied.

2. Swirl

Swirling the glass not only helps to aerate the wine before you sniff or taste it, but also helps you assess the viscosity and alcohol content of the wine. To keep control of the glass and not risk sloshing it all over the table, it's best to keep the glass on the table with your hand over the base and then swirl gently. Generally, the higher the alcohol content of a wine, the thicker and more viscous it is. The presence of wine 'legs' – the tear-like droplets that run down the inside of the glass after you've swirled it – is a good indicator of alcohol content. The more legs the wine has, the higher the alcohol content. Wine that coats the inside of the glass and appears syrupy when swirled is likely to be high in sugar.

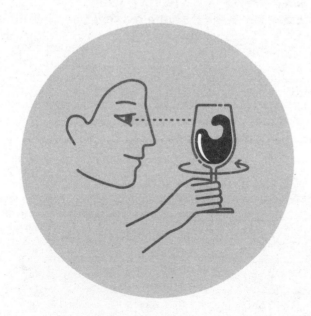

3. Smell

At least 50 per cent of the pleasure of drinking wine comes from the nose. I religiously nose my wine before every sip. Now the wine has been swirled, the glass should be ripe with delicious aromas. Hold your nose close to the mouth of the glass and inhale deeply to see what aromas you can detect. Use the bank of aromas that is stored in your memory as well as your imagination when you do this. Be free and confident – if you detect a smell it's because it is there! This will give you a good idea of whether the wine in the glass is likely to be fruity, herbal, flinty or earthy (think stable floor). If you detect notes of vanilla or spice, it's a good sign that the wine has been aged in oak and may be rich in tannins. This stage is also the first chance to detect if there is anything wrong with the wine – whether it is corked or overoxidized (see pages 34–5).

4. Taste

Finally, take a sip of the wine, sniffing again as you do so, then swill the wine around your mouth. Different zones of your tongue are better at detecting different flavours, so it's important to coat every side. If you're tasting red wine, it can be a good idea to suck some air through your teeth as you take your sip – this further helps aerate the wine and opens up the flavours in your mouth. Once you've swilled it around your mouth for a few seconds, swallow the wine and then take a deep breath, all the time thinking about the flavours now coating your tongue. Does the wine taste sweet or dry? Is it mellow or high in acid? Does it coat your tongue and have heft and body, or is it lighter? If it leaves your mouth feeling dry, this indicates a wine that's high in tannins. If the wine leaves a burn at the back of your throat then it is likely to have a high alcohol content. Most importantly, does it taste good? It is very rare to receive a corked wine, but it does happen. Trust your senses – if the wine smells or tastes musty, then it is likely to be bad.

Tasting notes

Use the terms below to talk about wine like a pro.

Acidic: If a wine tastes crisp and refreshing it is likely to be high in acid – think of the first bite of a particularly juicy apple. More prevalent in sparkling and white wines than reds. Acid is desirable to a degree, but wine that is overly acidic can taste vinegary or sour.

Alcohol: Wine with a higher alcohol content can leave a burning sensation at the back of your throat. Lower alcohol wines are softer on the palate.

Aroma: The unique smell of a wine, also referred to as the bouquet.

Astringency: Wine that is high in tannins are often described as being astringent. These wines can leave a mouth-puckering dryness in your mouth, similar to over-brewed tea.

Balance: All wine combines the four elements of acidity, sweetness, tannin and alcohol. Wines that meld the four in harmony are often described as well-balanced.

Body: The weight of the wine in your mouth and how it coats your tongue. Wines vary between being light-, medium- and full-bodied.

Bouquet: *See* Aroma.

Buttery: Often used to describe rich, creamy whites that are heavy in vanilla, nutty flavour and oak.

Cassis: Dark, blackcurrant flavours.

Chewy: Tannic without being overwhelmingly astringent. Chewy wines tend to be rich in fruit and full-bodied with an underlying hint of tannin.

Chocolatey: Rich wines that coat your mouth in a similar way to chocolate. Also reds that are rich with vanilla and spice, such as Syrah/Shiraz.

Closed: Wine that has full potential but is yet to realise it – like an unopened flower bud. Often benefits from aging or decanting.

Complexity: A wine with great complexity will have layers of flavour that reveal themselves through continued tasting.

Corked: Wine that smells and tastes musty due to cork taint (see page 23).

Crisp: Particularly refreshing, with just the right amount of acidity.

Dry: Wines with little residual sugar.

Earthy: Wines with a hint of mulch or ripe decay. Good in small amounts.

Expressive: Wine that is full of flavour and character.

Finish: The lasting impression left by a wine after you have swallowed.

Flabby: Lacking acidity and structure.

Flinty: White wines with a hint of minerality and a clean, almost metallic taste. Commonly used to describe Loire Valley whites, such as Sancerre and Pouilly-Fumé.

Fruity/Fruit-forward: Rich in fruit flavours, often berries (red wine) or orchard fruits (white wine).

Grapey: *See* Juicy.

Grassy: Smelling and tasting of grass or herbs, often used to describe Sauvignon Blanc.

Jammy: Red wine that is high in fruit and low in tannins.

Juicy: Tastes like grapes. Particularly young wines, such as Beaujolais Nouveau.

Mineral: *See* Flinty.

Oaky: Rich in vanilla spice and toasted nuts. Indicative of the wine having been stored in oak barrels.

Oxidized: Wine that has been over-exposed to air and lost its aroma.

Smooth: Well-rounded wine that is soft on the palate and light in tannins.

Spicy: Wine with hints of spice, which can vary from soft vanilla and nutmeg to black peppercorn and be the result of oak aging or the variety of grape used to make the wine.

Tannin/Tannic: Tannins are compounds found in the skin, seeds and stems of grapes, and are also found in the wood used to make oak casks. Wines that are overly tannic can taste astringent and somewhat bitter.

Tar: Wine with hints of tar, tobacco or liquorice. Often used to describe Italian Barolos, which are made from the Nebbiolo grape.

Tart: Wine with high acidity or mouth-puckering sourness. Hints of gooseberry or lemon.

Vegetal: Notes of vegetable that can indicate that the wine was made with underripe grapes.

Pairing wine with food

When writing this book I struggled with whether to include a section on food pairings at all. I knew that it would be expected and that not covering it would be seen as an omission, but I also know that great wine and great food will always be a happy match, whatever you're drinking or eating. When it comes to wine, nothing makes me more irritated than being told what I have to drink at a certain time. Wine is about enjoyment, not rules. Drink something because it will bring you happiness in that moment, not because I've told you that it will pair particularly well with your steak or bring out the sweetness in your strawberries. That said...

Some very informal guidelines on pairing wine and food

Keep it balanced
Light dishes with delicate flavours pair well with lighter wines. It's fine to have red wine with your fish, but keep it light and fruity rather than full-bodied and tannic. The idea is for the food and wine to complement each other, not for one to overshadow the other. Likewise, a rich steak pairs particularly well with a full-bodied red as the tannins in the wine help to cut through the richness of the meat and the fat in the meat softens the wine's astringency, but that's not to say that a full-bodied, oaky white can't do the same job.

Mix or match

With delicate flavours it's important to pick wine with complementary notes so as not to overshadow the food, but for more robust, flavour-rich foods, a contrasting flavour that juxtaposes the food can be even more exciting. As an example, dessert wines aren't just for dessert – pair them with rich, fatty foods, such as terrine or pâté, and they will refresh your palate and make the food sing.

Spice is nice

A pint of lager with a Friday night curry is a British institution and is perfect to glug if the spice gets the better of you, but give it a try and you'll find that wine and curry can also pair wonderfully. For milder, creamier curries, wines that are high in acid, such as a Riesling or Pinot Noir, will help to cleanse the palate between mouthfuls. For tomato-based curries that are rich in spice, choose a similarly spicy wine, such as a Grenache or Syrah, or even a rich, buttery Chardonnay if you're in the market for a white wine.

Say cheese

Wine and cheese are a match made in heaven, but depending on what's on your cheeseboard you may want to mix up what's in your glass. For example, if you're a fan of a wonderfully ripe Stilton, heavy with salt and acidic tang, then you need to pair it with a wine that can stand up to those flavours, which is why port and blue cheese is such a classic combination. Likewise, a silky chunk of Brie slides down wonderfully with a glug of Champagne to offset its richness.

Don't be bitter

If the food you're eating is sweeter than the wine that you're drinking, the wine can end up tasting bitter. This is the reason that dessert wines tend to be tooth-achingly sweet on their own, but paired with, say, a perfectly soft baked peach, they make perfect sense.

Ignore all the above and do what you want. It's what a Frenchman would do.

Know your grapes

With over 10,000 varieties of wine grapes around the world, gaining mastery of them can feel like an impossible task. The good news is that only a very small handful of these grapes make up the vast majority of wine produced, so knowing a little can get you a long way. Here I have chosen 12 of the most popular wine grapes from across the world to get you started: six white and six red. The same grapes grown in different countries and regions can take on vastly different characteristics, so when getting to know a particular varietal it can help to taste a broad spectrum of wines from different regions.

White wine grapes

Chardonnay

Originally from Burgundy, Chardonnay is now the most widely
grown white wine grape in the world and can be found in any
country where wine is produced. Because of its neutrality,
it is known as a winemaker's grape in that it acts as a blank
canvas for wine producers to paint upon. Wines made with
Chardonnay grapes run the spectrum from clean and flinty to
full-bodied and fruity, so there really is a Chardonnay to suit
every palate. Some wine drinkers proudly fall into the ABC
(Anything But Chardonnay) club, but this is usually a reaction
to the heavily oaked varieties common to California, which can
be overwhelming on the palate. Under questioning you will
usually find that these same people are more than happy to
quaff a glass of Chablis or Pouilly Fuissé, both of which are 100
per cent Chardonnay.

Chardonnay is one of the three varietals most commonly used
in Champagne production – if a Champagne is marked as *Blanc
de blancs* (white from whites) it is made with 100 per cent
Chardonnay grapes. The name refers to the fact that the other
grape varietals used in making Champagne, Pinot Noir and
Pinot Meunier, are both red.

Chenin Blanc

Native to the Loire Valley, Chenin Blanc grapes are now most
widely grown in South Africa, where it makes up around 20 per
cent of the annual grape crop. They are high in acidity and have
a honeyed, floral quality similar to Chardonnay. The grapes are
used to make wines that range from dry through to sweet, and
their high acidity makes them a good base for sparkling wines,
particularly the increasingly popular Crémant de Loire.

Pinot Grigio/Pinot Gris

This versatile white wine grape develops a pink tinge when
fully ripe. Most often associated with Italy, the grape actually
originates in Burgundy and is used in the Alsace region of France
to produce the late-harvest *vendanges tardives* dessert wines.
Classic examples of Pinot Grigio are often seen as entry-level,
easy-drinking wines as they are crisp, light and easy on the

palate. The grapes are high in sugar and low in acidity, and are suited to growing in cooler climates. In Italy, great examples can be found in the Friuli-Venezia Giulia region in the north-east of the country.

Riesling

Hailing from the Rhine region of Germany, Riesling grapes are very expressive of their *terroir* and are used to make wines that run the gamut from bone dry to very sweet. As a good indicator, wines with an ABV (alcohol percentage) of 12 per cent or higher tend to be drier, whereas lower-alcohol varieties are sweeter. Riesling is Germany's leading grape variety, but is also grown in the Alsace region of France and across Austria. Riesling wines are not known as easy drinkers, but have great range and complexity and can pair wonderfully with food. German Rieslings age well and are one of the few white wines that really benefit from being laid down for a few years. Outside of Europe, good examples of Riesling can be found in New York and Washington state.

Sauvignon Blanc

Originating from Bordeaux, Sauvignon Blanc is an aromatic, green-skinned grape that is now widely grown in wine regions across the world. Sauvignon Blanc wines are known for their high acidity and distinctive herbaceous flavour. In France the grapes are grown in both the Loire Valley and Bordeaux regions, though in Bordeaux they are most often blended with Sémillon grapes. Loire Valley Sauvignon Blancs such as Sancerre, Pouilly-Fumé and Quincy are notable for their grassy notes and flinty, mineral undertones, which are a result of the unique shell-laden limestone soil around the banks of the Loire River. Sauvignon Blanc grapes grown in the warmer climes of New Zealand, Australia and the Americas retain the grassy notes typical of the grape, but tend to be more pungent than French varieties, with tropical fruit flavours coming through.

Viognier

Originating from the Rhône region in south-eastern France, Viognier grapes are known for their distinctive perfumed quality. Viognier is now grown throughout the world, but thrives in warm climates such as the Rhône and Languedoc-Roussillon regions of France, California and southern Australia. It can be found as a single-varietal wine but is also commonly used in blended wines, mixed with Syrah, Marsanne or Chardonnay. In cooler climates Viognier exhibits floral citrus flavours, but grown in warmer regions reveals perfumed tropical fruit flavours.

Red wine grapes

Cabernet Sauvignon

Originating from Bordeaux, Cabernet Sauvignon is one of the most recognised and highly regarded grapes in the world. It is synonymous with Bordeaux wines, where it is grown along the left bank of the Gironde estuary, but it is found in winemaking regions globally. The grapes are relatively thick-skinned, resulting in wines that are high in tannins but develop wonderfully over time. Cabernet Sauvignon wines are rich in deep cassis and tobacco flavours and typically benefit from breathing time or decanting to allow the wine to open up. Outside of France, there are wonderful Cabernets in the USA, particularly the Napa Valley, where the unique climate gives the wine rich berry flavours. Along with Chardonnay, Cabernet wines were central in the famous Judgment of Paris in 1976, where Californian Cabernet Sauvignons beat classic French Bordeaux in a blind taste testing, making the world sit up and take wines from the USA seriously for the first time.

Merlot

Another grape hailing from Bordeaux, where it is often blended with Cabernet Franc for delicious results. Merlot is lighter in tannins than Cabernet Sauvignon, but has similar dark fruit flavours and notes of chocolate and vanilla, especially when aged in oak casks, making it a great option for those who are tannin averse. Because of the comparatively light tannins, Merlot matures in the bottle faster than Cabernet Sauvignon and can be drunk younger. Outside of France, Merlot is commonly used in the Italian 'Super Tuscan' wines (see pages 8–9) along with Cabernet Sauvignon, both non-native to Italy. Merlot is popular throughout the New World, particularly in the USA and Southern Australia.

Nebbiolo

This dark, thick-skinned grape from Piedmont is known for making the coveted tannin-rich wines of Barolo and Barbaresco. Wines made with these grapes can be overly astringent when young, but aged for several years unfold to be soft, supple and delicious with delicate cherry aromas. Nebbiolo is rarely grown outside of Italy, though examples can be found in the USA and Australia.

Pinot Noir

Known for fresh, fruity wines that are light in body and perfect for drinking on warm days, Pinot Noir grapes are native to Burgundy, but are also one of the three varietals used in the production of Champagne. Burgundy Pinot Noirs are regarded as some of the best wines in the world and examples from top producers can fetch very high prices. Their lighter body means that Pinot Noir wines benefit from light chilling and make a good companion to delicately flavoured foods, where other reds might overwhelm. Outside of France, it is the most widely grown red wine grape in New Zealand, where it develops distinctive mineral, potent fruit and subtle spice flavours.

Sangiovese

Originating from Tuscany, Sangiovese is one of Italy's best-known grapes, accounting for 10 per cent of all grapes grown in the country. It is also grown in South America, California and Australia. It is a hugely versatile grape and is used to make everything from classic reds to sparkling and dessert wines. It performs well in limestone soils and a warm, though not hot, climate. The grape has high acidity and it is often fermented for prolonged periods of time and heavily oaked to make it more palatable. Sangiovese is synonymous with the wines of Chianti, which are always made of at least 70 per cent of the wine. It is often used in blended Italian wines, and is a common base for Super Tuscan wines (see pages 8–9) when blended with Merlot or Cabernet Sauvignon.

Syrah/Shiraz

Originally from the Rhône region of south-east France, Syrah grapes produce full-bodied wines that are rich with fruit and spice, particularly black pepper. In France, wonderful examples of Syrah can be found in the Côte-Rôtie and Hermitage AOCs, both in the Northern Rhône region. It is the most widely grown red wine grape in Australia, where it is known as Shiraz, and produces some of the best varieties in the world, with Penfolds Grange being one of the most notable examples.

Wine rules and how to break them

One of the reasons that wine can seem intimidating is because it is mired in so many dated rules and people are afraid to experiment for fear of being judged. Now that we've covered the basics, you should have enough knowledge to realise that there is a lot of enjoyment to be found in colouring outside the lines. So throw the rulebook in the bin, stop worrying and start enjoying wine. To help you recap, here are some of those outdated wine rules and the best ways to break them.

1. White wine with fish, red wine with steak

Drink what you feel like in the moment. If you want to pair a red wine with fish, go for something light like a Pinot Noir or a Beaujolais. Likewise, try a rich, buttery Chardonnay with your steak.

2. Corks over screwcaps

While corks are great for full-bodied reds that benefit from a little aging, in almost every other circumstance a screwcap is just as good, and a lot more convenient.

3. Chilled white, warm red

Rather than thinking about colour, think about body. Lighter red wines benefit from a little chilling, fuller-bodied reds are best at room temperature, or just below. Overchilling white wine can kill delicate aromas; an hour or two in the fridge is just fine.

4. Red wines need decanting

There is no need to decant young reds that are light in tannins. Full-bodied, tannin-rich reds may benefit from being decanted, but be careful with older, more fragile wines that can oxidize quickly when exposed to air.

5. Champagne is only for celebrations

Make any day a celebration! Fizz works brilliantly with food and is a great choice when you're unsure of what to order in a restaurant. Champagne can be very expensive, especially in restaurants, but a bottle of Crémant can be every bit as delicious and makes a much cheaper alternative.

6. Use the right glass

If you have a selection of glassware for every occasion, good for you! For the rest of us, use whatever you have to hand.

7. Dessert wines with dessert

Sweet wines work well at the end of the meal with something sweet, but they are also brilliant palate cleansers when served with rich, fatty foods.

8. Good wine is expensive wine

Good wine is wine that tastes great and is enjoyed with wonderful company. Sometimes it's expensive, sometimes it's not!

PART TWO

Wine Regions

Now that we've got a good grasp of some wine fundamentals, it's time to take a tour of the world's most important winemaking nations. In this section of the book we will go country by country, looking at key regions and what they specialise in, so that you can start building an internal atlas and gain a greater understanding of how landscape, climate, tradition and grape varietal all play a vital part in what ends up in your glass.

In the past the world of wine has often been split into two clear categories: Old World and New World, with the Old World being dominated by European countries, such as France, Italy and Spain, with rich winemaking histories and, in many cases, more strictly governed rules around viticulture. The countries of the New World, such as Australia, New Zealand, the USA and South Africa, have often been seen as the young upstarts of winemaking, free from the strict rules and regulations of the Old World and often more experimental as a result. These lines are becoming more and more blurred, and categorising wine-producing countries in this way now feels out of date and slightly tainted by the snobbery that can pervade the wine world.

The modern world of wine shouldn't be about old and new, it should be about quality and enjoyment. In the last 30 years the world-shrinking power of the internet has opened up gateways for winemakers around the globe to share information about their practices and techniques and learn from one another: New from Old and Old from New. There are wonderful, joy-filled bottles of wine to be found the world over, each one a unique distillation of a certain place at a certain time. Go forth and explore.

Europe

Austria

Though not a major exporter of wine, Austria is known for its crisp, dry whites and for championing one signature grape varietal in particular, Grüner Veltliner, which accounts for around 40 per cent of all grapes grown in the country. Highly acidic and with clean notes of celery and white pepper, the wine can be made in a spectrum of styles and becomes increasingly full-bodied and aromatic with age.

You may remember the Austrian wine scandal in 1985, which uncovered the presence of diethylene glycol (a chemical component used in the production of antifreeze) in some of its wines produced for the German market. The scandal destroyed the Austrian wine industry overnight, but the intermittent years have seen small, quality-focused producers working hard to change the face of the Austrian wine industry and bring it back from the brink. Their hard work has paid off and Austria is now marked by consistently high-quality wines made by talented and passionate winemakers.

Though Grüner Veltliner is undoubtedly Austria's most famous export, there are over 30 different grape varietals approved for making wine in the country. These are generally made up of grapes that do well in Austria's cooler climate, such as Riesling for white wines, and native grapes such as Zweigelt and Blaufränkisch for red wines.

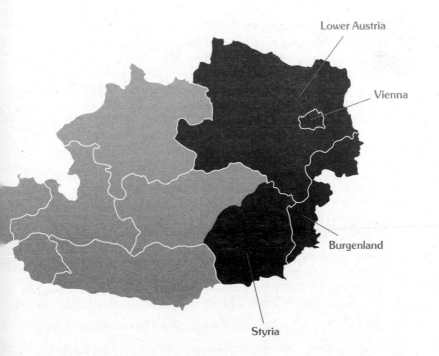

Lower Austria

Vienna

Burgenland

Styria

Austrian Wine Classifications

Somewhat confusingly, there are several separate wine classification systems at play in Austria. In response to the wine scandal of 1985, production of wine in Austria became more closely monitored and, after Austria joined the EU in 1995, an appellation system was soon introduced that closely governed the grapes grown and production practices within key geographical areas. Rather than the appellation system replacing what was already in play, the systems overlaid each other, meaning that the various terminologies and classification styles can be initially confusing.

National Classification

Austria's national classification system is based on ripeness and residual sugar in harvested grapes. Wines are graded on the Klosterneuburg Weight Scale (KMW), which measures grams of sugar per 100g of grape must (unfermented grape juice). The idea is that wines with a higher KMW rating are of a higher quality and need less interference in terms of adding sugar (a method known as chaptalization) during the fermenting process. Going from highest to lowest quality, the rankings for wine using this classification are:

Prädikatswein – This tier is used to classify Austria's late-harvest sweet wines. This level is divided into several sub-categories, all with specific KMW ratings and rules on when grapes can be harvested.

Qualitätswein – 15°KMW is the minimum naturally occurring sugar for wines to qualify in this category, but they can be chaptalized to 19°KMW for white wines and 20°KMW for reds. Grapes must originate from a single recognised wine district.

Landwein – 14°KMW. Region of origin must be on the label.

Wein – 10.6°KMW. These wines need to be heavily chaptalized to make them palatable.

DAC Classification

Austria's appellation system was introduced in 2001 and is known as the Districtus Austriae Controllatus (DAC). The DAC system is overlayed with the National Classification system, so any wine with a DAC designation on the label also meets the quality markers for a top-tier of Qualitätswein under the National Classification system.

There are 16 DAC appellations in Austria and each has a list of approved grapes that can be grown within its boundaries and used in its wines. Though DAC laws must conform to those set by the EU and the National Classification system, they are set locally by regional committees and are often more stringent than they have to be; this can be seen as part of Austria's drive to reposition the country as one of the foremost producers of consistently high-quality wines.

Austrian wine regions

Burgenland

Situated on Austria's eastern border with Hungary, Burgenland is home to the majority of Austria's red wine production, of which Zweigelt and Blaufränkisch are its signature grapes. The region enjoys hot, dry summers that are well-suited to ripening red wine grapes. The sub-region of Mittelburgenland, where vines sit on the lower climes of the Ödenburg Mountains, produces some particularly fine examples of Blaufränkisch.

The region includes four DAC appellations, including Neusiedlersee, which is famous for producing high-quality sweet white wines that fall into the category of Prädikatswein (see above). The other DAC appellations in the region are Leithaberg, Eisenberg and the aforementioned Mittelburgenland. It is worth noting that wine that is labelled as Burgenland and does not include a specific DAC does not conform to the quality standards of the region.

Varietals permitted in Burgenland DAC wines

White
Grüner Veltliner
Müller Thurgau
Muskateller (Muscat)
Riesling
Chardonnay
Sauvignon Blanc

Red
Blaufränkisch
Zweigelt
St Laurent
Pinot Noir

Lower Austria

Lower Austria, or Niederösterreich, is situated in the northeast of the country, bordering Slovakia and the Czech Republic. It is known for its cool, dry climate that is perfect for growing Grüner Veltliner and Riesling grapes, which make up most of the region's output.

The region contains six DACs: Carnuntum, Kamptal, Kremstal, Traisental, Weinviertel and Wachau. Of these, Wachau has only recently been granted DAC status despite being one of Austria's most highly regarded white wine regions. Perhaps unhelpfully, Wachau uses its own classification system to grade its wines that can be further overlayed with the DAC system.

Wachau Classification

The Wachau classification system is set out by the Vinea Wachau Nobilis Districtus organisation, which closely monitors and protects wines produced in the region. Wines are categorised by style from light and refreshing to full-bodied and alcoholic. A wine that receives any of these gradings can be regarded as a high-quality option, though the fuller-bodied, more alcoholic wines are the most revered.

Steinfeder – a light and refreshing style of wine with a maximum alcohol content of 11.5% ABV.

Federspiel – Slightly more full-bodied wines with a raised alcohol content of up to 12.5% ABV.

Smaragd – Full-bodied, aromatic wines with an alcohol content of at least 12.5%. These wines can benefit from light aging to open up their flavour and reveal hidden depths.

Varietals permitted in Lower Austria DAC wines

White
Grüner Veltliner
Riesling
Müller-Thurgau
Muskateller (Muscat)
Pinot Blanc
Pinot Gris

Red
Blaufränkisch
Zweigelt

Styria

Also known as Steiermark, Styria is Austria's smallest and most southerly wine-producing region. It has a cool climate that sets it apart from other Austrian winemaking areas and is known for producing high-quality Sauvignon Blanc and sparkling wine, the latter made from the region's most widely grown grape, Welschriesling.

Styria accounts for under 10 per cent of Austria's wine output and includes three DAC appellations: Weststeiermark, Südsteiermark and Vulkanland Steiermark. Of these, Südsteiermark DAC is the easiest to seek out as it accounts for over half of the region's wine production, though it is worth searching for Sauvignon Blanc from Vulkanland Steiermark, which produces highly regarded examples that are very expressive of the region's *terroir*. Weststeiermark is notable for producing a strawberry-rich rosé known as Schilcher, made from Wildbacher grapes.

Varietals permitted in Styria DAC wines

White
Pinot Blanc
Chardonnay
Pinot Gris
Sauvignon Blanc
Muskateller (Muscat)
Gewürztraminer

Red
Wildbacher

Vienna

Austria's capital city of Vienna is surrounded on all sides by vineyards that make up the wine region of the same name. The wine of the region is heavily influenced by the Danube River, which snakes its way through Vienna and brings mineral-rich soils along its banks.

Vienna's sole DAC is Wiener Gemischter Satz, which is known for producing blended white wines. These wines are dry, unoaked and easy to drink, and are often made up of a combination of Grüner Veltliner, Riesling and Gewürztraminer. Under the rules of the DAC, the grapes are grown, harvested and vinified together, and no one grape varietal may account for more than 50 per cent of the grapes used to produce the wine.

Many Viennese wines are made to be drunk young. Each year on November 11th, the new season's wine is put on sale and sold in *Heurigers* (taverns) throughout the city, where the wine is enjoyed with food and music. Most of these wines are made from the region's white grapes; red varieties are also available, though it should be noted that none are grown in Vienna's sole DAC appellation, which focuses on white blends only. This celebration of young Viennese wine is very much part of the culture of Vienna and, though the wine may not always be the most refined, the atmosphere of civilised celebration and the glimpse into Viennese life is a real privilege to be a part of.

Varietals permitted in Vienna DAC wines

White
Grüner Veltliner
Riesling
Gewürztraminer
Chardonnay
Pinot Blanc

France

There is evidence of grape fermentation in Georgia as early as 6000 BC, but when wine arrived in France with Greek settlers in 600 BC it found its spiritual home. No other country has been so influential in the development of modern winemaking techniques, or shaped the history of wine so dramatically. France and wine simply go together.

Because of France's diverse landscape and varied climate, the wines made up and down the country vary wildly and each area specialises in the production of wines unique to themselves. This impact of landscape and climate imprinting on the taste of what ends up in your glass is tied to the concept of *terroir*, which is central to French winemaking. The *terroir* of an area is the cumulation of everything from the unique make-up of the soil and what grapes are grown in it, to the weather, geographical location and the way the grapes are handled after they have been harvested.

The *terroir* of an area leaves its mark on the wine that is made there and, to the trained palate, all of these elements are detectable in the glass. It is this celebration and protection of regional identity that makes French wine so special. When compared to those of younger winemaking countries, the rules that govern French wine may seem a little strict and stuffy, but it is precisely these rules that have led to France producing some of the world's finest wine, and being the first place that the rest of the world looks to for winemaking expertise.

Burgundy

The Loire Valley

Champagne

Alsace

Jura

The Rhône Valley

Bordeaux

Cahors

Provence

Languedoc-Roussillon

French Wine Classifications

French wine production is closely regulated and all wine produced in France falls into one of the three categories outlined below:

AOC (Appellation d'origine contrôlée)

This is the top level of French wine classification. There are over 300 recognised wine appellations in France, each with its own particular rules and each sitting in its own clearly demarked geographical area. Wine marked with the AOC designation must be made with grapes that are both 100 per cent grown within and only from the approved grape varietals for that particular appellation, as well as conforming to the rules on wine production within that area. Wines of this type are also sometimes labelled as AOP (Appellation d'origine protégée), but both AOC and AOP signify the same level of quality. AOC wines are tied to the French idea of *terroir* and are so highly regarded because they are reliably consistent and, as a result, of high quality.

IGP (Indication géographique protégée)

This middle tier of French wines, also sometimes referred to as *Vin de Pays*, is subject to a looser set of rules than AOC wines, but is still locked to specific geographical areas, though they tend to be larger and include a wider range of grape varietals. Production methods are not so tightly controlled, meaning that producers can be more experimental than in AOC areas. This can lead to the production of some very exciting wines, but also means that quality can vary widely.

Vin de France

Wines labelled as vin de France can be made from grapes grown anywhere in the country, with no limits on provenance or production techniques outside of the wine being safe to drink. These are generally the lowest-quality wines on the market, though exceptions can be found in areas that do not have IPG classification where winemakers want to experiment outside of the constraints of AOC rules.

French wine regions

Alsace

Unique among French wine regions, the wines of Alsace are labelled by varietal (see pages 7–8) rather than by appellation. This style of labelling is traditional to Germany (Alsace sits right on the French–German border, in the east of France). The Germanic influence on Alsace wines is also evident in the grapes that are grown in the region, such as Riesling and Gewürztraminer, though Alsace wines combine French production techniques with Germanic grapes to produce wines that are entirely unique (for example, Alsace Rieslings tend to be much drier than their German counterparts). The vast majority of the wines produced in Alsace are white, with Pinot Noir being the only grape permitted to be grown for AOC wines in the region.

Despite being situated in the north-east of France, the Alsace region is blessed with an abundance of sunshine, and sheltered from rain and wind by the Vosges Mountains to the west, making the climate ideal for slow-ripening grape varieties that thrive in long, dry summers. This mild climate is the reason that Alsace is also known for its dessert and late-harvest wines, where grapes are left on the vine longer to intensify their sugar content.

Varietals permitted in Alsace AOC wines

White
Auxerrois
Chasselas
Chardonnay (only when used
   in Crémant d'Alsace)
Gewürztraminer
Klevener de Heiligenstein
Muscat
Pinot Blanc
Pinot Gris
Riesling
Silvaner

Red
Pinot Noir

Bordeaux

Home to some of the most revered wines in the world, Bordeaux is known for gutsy, flavourful reds that develop brilliantly over time. Situated in the south-west of France with the Atlantic Ocean to the west, Bordeaux is bisected by three rivers: the Dordogne, the Garonne and the Gironde estuary. Wines from the area are often described as being from the right or left bank, referring to the location of the vineyards in relation to these rivers. Those produced to the right of the Gironde estuary and north of the Dordogne are right bank (e.g. Pomerol and St-Emilion), whereas those to the left of the Gironde estuary and south of the Garonne are left bank (e.g. Médoc, Margaux and Graves). To complicate matters further, wines produced in the triangular area between the Dordogne and the Garonne are known as *Entre-Deux-Mers* (meaning 'between two tides'), referring to the fact that the area sits between two tidal rivers. Though Bordeaux is primarily known for its red wines, the *Entre-Deux-Mers* area does not contain an AOC for red wines and is generally given over to growing white grape varietals such as Sauvignon Blanc and Sémillon.

Left versus right bank

The wonderful reds that Bordeaux is known for are produced on either the left or right bank of the Gironde estuary. Though most Bordeaux wine contains a blend of red grapes, left-bank wines generally contain a higher proportion of Cabernet Sauvignon whereas right-bank wines are higher in Merlot. The reason for these variations lies in the soil; the left bank of the Gironde has gravelly soil that is rich in limestone and better suited to Cabernet Sauvignon grapes, while the right-bank soil is finer and better suited to Merlot. Because Cabernet Sauvignon grapes are thick-skinned and high in tannins, left-bank wines tend to be better when aged. Right-bank Bordeaux wines can generally be drunk younger.

Bordeaux classifications

Here things get a bit more complicated. There are six different classification systems at play in Bordeaux, the most famous and influential being the 1855 classification of Bordeaux, which covers only left-bank wines from the Medoc region. This classification was requested by Emperor Napoleon III for the 1855 *Exposition Universelle* in Paris as a means of ranking Bordeaux wines and showing them off to the world. The vineyards in the region were broken down into *crus* (or 'growths'), and ranked, with Grands Cru being at the top. The Grands Crus were those whose wines showed the greatest expression of *terroir* at the time, and the rankings have not changed since. As a result, Bordeaux wines from Grands Cru wine estates, of which there are only five, are among the most expensive wines in the world, even today. These are:

- Château Haut-Brion
- Château Lafite Rothschild
- Château Latour
- Château Margaux
- Château Mouton Rothschild

If you are ever lucky enough to sample wine from any of these châteaus then you are surely in for a treat. It's important, however, to realise that this classification only includes wines from a tiny fraction of the Bordeaux region and there are many other delicious Bordeaux wines that can be purchased for a fraction of the price that these Grands Cru wines can fetch. Look to the left-bank appellations, particularly Pauillac AOC, which, as well as being home to three of the Grands Crus châteaus, also produces some more affordable examples that are still exceptionally high in quality. Château Duhart-Milon, Château Batailley and Château d'Armailhac are all good places to start.

Varietals permitted in Bordeaux AOC wines

White	Red
Sémillon	Merlot
Sauvignon Blanc	Cabernet Sauvignon
Muscadelle	Cabernet Franc
Colombard	Carménère
Merlot Blanc	Malbec
Sauvignon Gris	
Petit Verdot	
Ugni Blanc	

Burgundy

One of France's best-known wine regions, Burgundy is celebrated for its light Pinot Noirs and crisp Chardonnays, though other grapes, such as Gamay, also play a part. The area is also known for Crémant de Bourgogne sparkling wine, a delicious, buttery fizz that makes a wonderful and economical alternative to Champagne. As a rule of thumb, wines labelled as white Burgundy will be Chardonnay, and red Burgundy will be Pinot Noir.

Situated in the east of the country, between Champagne and the Rhône Valley, Burgundy is divided into five key wine producing areas: Chablis, Côte de Nuits, Côte de Beaune, Côte Chalonnaise and Mâconnais. Of these areas, Chablis is possibly the most famous, with many drinkers who would turn their nose up at anything labelled Chardonnay eagerly quaffing a glass of Chablis. The reason for this may be that the cool climate of the area results in Chardonnay grapes that have a crisp acidity and mineral notes that set them apart from other Chardonnays. Chablis is hardly ever oaked, so is a very pure expression of the Chardonnay grape, and one that has found many fans.

For red wine, look to the Côte de Nuits, which gives over 90 per cent of its production to Pinot Noir and contains many of the region's Grands Cru vineyards.

Burgundy classifications
Burgundy vineyards, also known as *Climat* or *Clos*, are ranked into one of four categories: Grands Cru, Premier Cru, Village and Regional. Burgundy Grands Cru make up a very small proportion of Burgundy wines, covering just over 30 vineyards across the Chablis, Côte de Nuits and Côte de Beaune areas. Each Grands Cru vineyard has been awarded its own AOC, so both the Grands Cru and AOC should be clearly visible on the label.

What about Beaujolais?

Beaujolais wines are often treated as separate to Burgundies, though they are produced within the same administrative area. The reason for this is that the wines of the Beaujolais region, which sits just to the south of Burgundy, are distinct from the rest of the region. Red Beaujolais steps away from the Pinot Noir that dominates the rest of the region and instead is made exclusively from Gamay grapes. White Beaujolais is made from Chardonnay, though the region is dominated by red production. Red Beaujolais wines are notable for their very low tannins and intense fruit flavours, with the most renowned being Beaujolais Nouveau, a style of wine which is designed to be sold and drunk in the same year that it is made. Full of vibrant berry fruit flavours and very light on the palate, Beaujolais Nouveau is put on sale on the third Thursday of November every year, just a couple of months after the grapes are first harvested.

Varietals permitted in Burgundy AOC wines

White
Chardonnay
Aligoté
Sauvignon Blanc

Red
Pinot Noir
Gamay (mainly Beaujolais)

Cahors

Found along the banks of the River Lot in the south-west of France, wine that is labelled as Cahors is at least 80 per cent Malbec. Malbec grapes thrive in the region's temperate climate, and the wine produced here is dark red, full-bodied and brimming with the flavours of ripe berry fruit. Cahors wines are rich with tannin and can benefit from aging for a few years to allow the wine to open up, though some producers have started to harvest grapes younger, resulting in wines with less tannin.

Cahors was not granted its own AOC until 1971, and historically its dark wines were blended with Bordeaux wines in years of poor growth. Three-quarters of the vineyards in the area are privately owned and the majority of the wine produced in Cahors is consumed in France, which helps explain why wines from this region are not as well known outside of the country as those from other regions.

The River Lot carves a meandering swathe through the landscape of the region, and the vineyards that grow along its banks are situated in varying landscapes and soils, from flat plateaus to steep hillsides. The closer the grapes are grown to the river, the more alluvial the soil, meaning it is composed of a mixture of loose sediment and mineral deposits that is highly prized by winemakers. The climate changes from Mediterranean (in the east) to more Atlantic (in the west), with relatively high rainfall. These fluctuations in landscape and climate mean that Cahors wines express their *terroir* in a significant manner and, though made from the same grape, the taste of Cahors wines can vary significantly depending on where in the region they are produced.

Varietals permitted in Cahors AOC wines

Red
Malbec   Merlot   Tannat

Champagne

There are many different styles of delicious sparkling wine in the world, but Champagne reigns supreme among them all. Situated to the east of Paris, Champagne production is grouped around the cities Épernay and Reims, and many of the well-known Champagne producers will feature one of these cities on their labels. Champagne is France's northernmost wine region and therefore one of the coldest. Historically, these low temperatures meant that winemakers struggled to ripen their grapes, resulting in wines that were highly acidic and unpalatable. To counter this, producers experimented with bottling wines before the first fermentation was complete and adding sugar before sealing to induce a second fermentation (more on the *méthode traditionnelle* used in Champagne production on page 5). This second fermentation in the bottle meant that the gases that formed had no means of escape and the resulting wines were fizzy. Thus Champagne was born.

The grapes used in making Champagne are usually a *cuvée* (blend) of Pinot Noir, Pinot Meunier and Chardonnay. Pinot Noir and Pinot Meunier are red-skinned grapes but yield a white wine in Champagne production as the skins are only lightly pressed. There are three other white grapes permitted to be used in the making of Champagne (see table on page 74), but they are very rarely used. Champagne that is made from a blend of just Pinot Noir and Pinot Meunier with no Chardonnay included is known as *Blanc de noirs* (white from blacks), whereas wines made with just Chardonnay are known as *Blanc de blancs* (white from whites). Rosé Champagnes are made by blending a small amount of red wine (also made from either Pinot Noir or Pinor Meunier) to the mix.

Champagne classifications

Because of the challenges of growing grapes in a cooler climate, the vintage or year the grapes are grown is crucial when looking for a great Champagne. Grapes harvested in years that have ideal growing conditions will yield superior wines, and wines labelled with these vintages are made entirely from grapes grown in these years and can fetch far higher prices. Most Champagnes are 'non-vintage', with grapes making it from vine to bottle in the same year that they are grown or being blended from multiple years. However, Champagne houses do keep a stock of wine from vintage years to blend with non-vintage Champagnes to improve their flavour. The Champagne industry is one of the very few that can be said to be benefiting from the climate change crisis, as the gradual increase in temperature means that vintage years with milder weather are becoming more and more regular.

The Cru system in the Champagne region differs from others in that it focuses on the villages where grapes are grown within the region, rather than grading the vineyards themselves. Known as the *échelle des crus* (ladder of growth), the system gives each village a grading between 1 and 100, with only those that score a perfect 100 being designated as Grands Cru. Those that score 90 and above are designated as Premier Cru, and the remaining villages do not have an official designation. There are over 300 wine-growing villages in the region and only 17 of these are classified as Grands Cru and 44 as Premier Cru. A wine labelled as either Grands Cru or Premier Cru can achieve higher prices as a result.

Many will know Champagne as being crisp and dry, though it does in fact range between *Brut Sauvage* (very dry) and *Doux* (very sweet). What most people think about when they imagine sipping on a glass of chilled Champagne (and the majority sold), is labelled as *Brut* (dry).

Varietals permitted in Champagne AOC wines

White
Chardonnay (*Cuvée/Blanc de blancs*)
Arbane (rarely used)
Pinot Gris (rarely used)
Pinot Blanc (rarely used)
Petit Meslier (rarely used)

Red
Pinot Noir (*Cuvée/Blanc de noirs*)
Pinot Meunier (*Cuvée/Blanc de noirs*)

Jura

This small and relatively unknown winemaking region can be found to the east of Burgundy, on France's border with Switzerland. The vast majority of the wines produced here are consumed in France rather than exported, which in some way explains how wines from the region are not that well known outside of France.

The signature grape of the region is Savagnin Blanc (not to be confused with Sauvignon Blanc), which is used to produce *Vin Jaune* (yellow wine), a sweet wine made with late-harvest grapes in a winemaking style that is unique to the region, though most closely resembles Portugal's traditional methods for producing sherries.

Another wine style that is unique to the area is Macvin, a sweet wine made from either white or red grapes. It has a high alcohol percentage (around 20% ABV) due to the addition of *Eau-de-vie de marc*, a spirit that is distilled from the grape pulp, skins and seeds that are left over after being pressed for wine production.

The third signature wine style from the Jura region is *Vin de Paille* (straw wine), which is made from Chardonnay, Savagnin Blanc and Poulsard grapes that have been cut from the vine and then left to dry for around three months. This process results in a dessert wine with a rich amber colour, high residual sugar and the perfumed flavour of ripe stone fruits.

Varietals permitted in Jura AOC wines

White	Red
Chardonnay	Poulsard
Savagnin Blanc	Pinot Noir
	Trousseau

Languedoc-Roussillon

Situated in south-west France, Languedoc-Roussillon is the country's largest winemaking region. This grand size has not always been to the region's benefit and it is known for producing large volumes of fairly mediocre wine, though with a little searching you can find some very special wines here.

The climate and geography of the region are highly advantageous for growing grapes – with the Mediterranean coast bringing warm sea breezes and soil made up of limestone, gravel or, closer to the coast, layers of seashell – meaning that grapes of many varieties thrive here. Indeed, unlike other winemaking regions in France, where the region on the bottle is enough to tell the informed drinker what grapes their wine is made up of, AOC wines from Languedoc-Roussillon can be made from any of around 30 different grape varietals; at IGP level (see page 64) this number goes up to around 50.

The proliferation of grape varietals means that the area is known for its blends, with the rich liquorice flavours of Syrah and Grenache forming the base of many quality reds. Single-varietal wines can be found in the region, with Picpoul de Pinet becoming an increasingly popular alternative to the more obvious Sauvignon Blancs and Pinot Grigios for those looking for a crisp and refreshing white wine. When it comes to sparkling wine, the region's Crémant de Limoux, made with a blend of Chardonnay and Chenin Blanc grapes, makes a delicious and more affordable alternative to Champagne.

Common varietals in Languedoc-Roussillon wines

White
Bourboulenc
Clairette
Grenache Blanc
Macabeo
Malvoisie du Roussillon/Tourbat
Marsanne
Mauzac
Muscat à Petits Grain
Muscat d'Alexandrie
Picpoul Blanc
Roussanne
Terret Blanc
Ugni Blanc
Vermentino

Red
Carignan
Cinsault
Gamay
Grenache
Lledoner Pelut
Mourvèdre
Syrah

The Loire Valley

Situated towards the north of France and grouped along its longest river, the Loire, this region is large and spans several sub-regions, each with its own distinctive characteristics and winemaking traditions. The Loire Valley is made up of 87 different AOC appellations, divided between the upper, middle and lower Loire. The lower Loire, situated on the Atlantic coast, has a moderate, even climate with cool summers and mild winters, whereas the middle and upper Loire regions, situated towards the centre of the country, enjoy warm summers but cold winters.

The lower Loire is known for its white Muscadet wines produced around the city of Nantes. Any wine labelled as Muscadet will be made exclusively from Melon de Bourgogne grapes and will be light-bodied, crisp and fresh, often with a slightly perfumed, yeasty aroma said to be reminiscent of melon, hence the name of the grape. Despite there being some delicious varieties available, Muscadet wines have not broken through into the public consciousness and good examples can be picked up relatively cheaply.

Move eastward along the Loire river and you reach the middle Loire, which includes the sub-regions Chinon, Touraine, Saumur and Vouvray and dominated by Chenin Blanc and Cabernet Franc grapes. Wines from these areas are characterised by high acidity. Though the region is best known for its white wines, Touraine AOC is notable for producing a small amount of Malbec wine under the regional name of Côt. Anjou, Touraine and Cheverny are also known for their excellent sparkling Crémant de Loire wines.

The upper Loire is home to two AOCs that are perhaps the best known in the Loire Valley – Sancerre and Pouilly-Fumé. Both of these areas are known for producing exceptional Sauvignon Blanc wines with high acidity and a distinctive gunflint note that comes from the flinty soil of the area. These wines can be more expensive than other varieties of Sauvignon Blanc, but are unique for their clean mineral notes and grassy undertones that separate them from the more fruit-forward Sauvignon Blancs found elsewhere.

Varietals permitted in Loire Valley AOC wines

White
Arbois
Chardonnay
Chasselas
Chenin Blanc
Folle Blanche
Melon de Bourgogne
Pinot Gris
Romorantin
Sauvignon Blanc
Sacy

Red
Cabernet Franc
Cabernet Sauvignon
Gamay
Grolleau
Malbec
Pineau d'Aunis
Pinot Meunier
Pinot Noir

Provence

Home to some of France's most beautiful landscapes, Provence is situated on France's Mediterranean coast in the far south-east of France. Its climate is characterised by long, hot summers and mild winters, so it's no wonder that its most famous wine is often seen as a summer drink – Provence means pink! The region produces 40 per cent of all France's rosé, and in recent years the area has been at the centre of a revolution in the reputation in this style of wine. The rosé produced here is crisp, pale, acidic, dry and refreshing, and a far cry from the overly sweet, perfumed rosés that have dominated supermarket shelves in the past.

The key grape used to make Provencal rosé is Cinsault, which grows well in the limestone-heavy soil of the region. The generous sunshine and cool sea breezes create a constant climate in the region, which produces consistently superior wines.

One of the most famous AOCs in the area is Bandol, which is famous for its red and rosé wines. Bandol rosés – primarily made from Mourvèdre grapes but often with the inclusion of Grenache and Cinsault – are prized for their clean minerality and light, fresh flavour, which make them perfect on hot summer days. Bandol is also famous for its spicy red wines, also made from at least 50 per cent Mourvèdre. While red wine used to dominate production in Bandol AOC, in recent years production has shifted to 70 per cent rosé. Though fashion definitely plays a key part in this, this can also be attributed to the fact that reds from the region need to be aged for significant times in oak casks, whereas rosés here are bottled and sold without aging and fetch a similarly high price, making them a much more attractive and labour-light option for producers.

Varietals permitted in Provence AOC wines

White
Vermentino (Rolle)
Ugni Blanc
Bourboulenc
Clairette
Marsanne
Roussanne
Grenache Blanc

Red
Grenache
Syrah (Shiraz)
Mourvèdre
Carignan
Cinsault
Counoise
Tannat
Cabernet Sauvignon

The Rhône Valley

One of France's oldest wine-producing regions, the Rhône Valley, situated in the south-east of the country, can be split into two distinct regions, the Northern Rhône and the Southern Rhône, both of which lie along the banks of the Rhône River.

Grapes grown in the Northern Rhône are limited to only four varietals: Syrah (red), Marsanne (white), Roussane (white) and Viognier (white). Wines here are usually single varietals or uncomplicated blends. Red wines from the region can be blended with a little white wine (Marsanne or Roussanne) to soften the tannins from the thick-skinned Syrah grapes. Of the white wines produced here, Condrieu, made from 100 per cent Viognier grapes, is among the best regarded and is worth seeking out.

The Southern Rhône is slightly more complex. Whereas grapes in the Northern Rhône are grown on steep terraces along the banks of the river, those in the south are generally situated further from the river on flat plateaus that are suited to growing a wider range of grape varietals. As a consequence of this, there are over 20 different varietals grown in the Southern Rhône, as opposed to just four in the Northern area of the region. This proliferation of grape varietals means that this region is known for its blends. Reds make up 85 per cent of the wine produced in the Southern Rhône, with Grenache taking centre stage in many of the best-regarded wines. As a result of this, red wines from the south tend to be lighter than those from the north (where Syrah is king). Only 5 per cent of wine produced here is white, with the remaining 10 per cent being made up of rosé wines, particularly in the Tavel appellation, which is entirely given over to rosé.

Wines that are labelled as Côtes du Rhône can come from anywhere within the Rhône Valley. Wines labelled as Côtes du Rhône Villages tend to be slightly higher quality than those without the 'Villages' designation, and if this labelling is paired with the name of an individual village, then it is a good indicator of a high-quality wine, as only a handful of villages within the region have permission to include their name on the label.

One of the best-known appellations within the Southern Rhône is Châteauneuf-du-Pape, known for its Grenache-based red wines of exceptionally high quality. It is a misconception (perhaps boosted by the 'château' part of the area's name) that a single producer is responsible for all of these wines; in fact, it is a whole area, named after the ruined papal castle of Pope John XXII.

Varietals permitted in Rhône Valley AOC wines

Northern Rhône

White	Red
Marsanne	Syrah
Roussanne	
Viognier	

Southern Rhône

White	Red
Bourboulenc	Brun Argenté
Clairette Blanche	Carignan
Clairette Rose	Cinsault
Grenache Blanc	Counoise
Grenache Gris	Grenache Noir
Marsanne	Marselan
Piquepoul Blanc	Mourvèdre
Roussanne	Muscardin
Ugni Blanc	Piquepoul Noir
Viognier	Syrah
	Terret Noir

Germany

Germany is one the world's most northern wine-producing countries and is known for its cool climate and long growing season. Grapes that are grown here take on the unique characteristics of the landscape because the grapes spend so long on the vine.

This means that German wines are often highly aromatic and very distinctive to those made from the same grapes elsewhere, with some high-quality German wines being noted for their high levels of precision and clarity. Wine from Germany is largely produced in the west of the country, with vineyards following the route of the Rhine River as it wends through the landscape.

Known primarily for its white wines, with Riesling being the most common varietal in the country, Germany is also one of the world's most prolific producers of Pinot Noir, where it is sold as Spätburgunder.

Rheingau

Mittelrhein

Ahr

Mosel Valley

Franken

Nahe

Rheinhessen

Pflalz

Baden

German wine classifications

For those who have a good understanding of French or Italian wine laws, where *terroir* and geographic indication are closely tied to the quality grading that a wine is awarded, German wine rules can be a little difficult to get a handle on. The German system is influenced heavily by the German wine law reform of 1971, which sought to shift the focus away from the specific landscape that grapes were grown in and instead focused on how ripe the grapes were at the time of harvest.

The reason for this was that Germany viewed the French and Italian systems as elitist, believing that those who happened to be lucky enough to own land in top-tier AOC (France) or DOCG (Italy) areas could charge much more for their wine simply by virtue of their location, whereas those in areas with growing conditions that weren't as highly regarded could never reach these heights. The 1971 law sought to give all German producers the chance to reach these higher levels.

The focus on grape ripeness as a quality indicator is tied to the fact that Germany's climate is generally cooler than that of other winemaking countries, meaning ripening grapes takes far longer. Wine made with underripe grapes typically must undergo chaptalization (where sugar is added to boost the fermentation process), whereas wine made with ripe grapes with good residual sugar will not need any sugar added and is therefore considered to be higher quality.

In 2009, the German grading system was brought in line with the rules that govern all wine produced in EU member countries. As such, German wines now all fall into one of the following three classifications:

Geschützte Ursprungsbezeichnung (gU)

This is the highest tier of German winemaking. Because the rules around viticulture are much looser in Germany than other European countries and grape ripeness is the metric required to reach this classification, the vast majority (90 per cent) of German wine falls into this category. Wines in this class must have a geographical identifier on the label and the grapes used in producing the wine must all be grown within this area.

Geschützte geographische Angabe (ggA)

This mid-level classification of German wine has a raised requirement for grape ripeness compared to the bottom tier, though wines in this category will also have sugar added during the winemaking process. At least 85 per cent of grapes used in production of this band of wines must be grown in one of Germany's 26 permitted *landwein* regions, which are grape-growing areas larger than those indicated on gU labels.

Wein

The lowest classification of German wine has a very low threshold for grape ripeness, and wines in this category will almost universally be made with added sugars to help the fermentation process. This wine is rarely exported outside of Germany.

German wine regions

Ahr

Germany's northernmost winemaking region, Ahr is also one of the country's smallest. Vineyards are nestled against the steep banks of the Ahr River, a left tributary of the mighty Rhine. Despite its northerly position, the planting of vineyards on the steep slopes surrounding the Ahr valley provides a mild microclimate that is suitable for growing red-wine grapes, which account for 80 per cent of the harvest there.

Because Ahr is a small region with a correspondingly small output, wines from the region can be quite expensive when compared to those from other areas in Germany. That's not to say that they're not worth the money; there are some wonderful examples to be found, though you may have to search as only a small percentage of Ahr wines are sold into the international market.

For the red wines that the area is known for, look for Spätburgunder (Pinot Noir), which accounts for over 60 per cent of all grapes grown in the region, or Frühburgunder, which is an early-ripening mutation of the Pinot Noir grape that thrives in Germany's cooler climate. These wines are often brick red with notes of cherry and an underlying hint of moss.

The region is less well known for its white wines, but just under 10 per cent of the area's output is given over to producing Riesling. These wines vary in flavour, from the refreshing notes of citrus in grapes grown in sunnier areas, to the clean and mineralistic profile of those grown in shadier spots.

Common varietals in Ahr wines

White
Riesling
Müller-Thurgau

Red
Spätburgunder
Frühburgunder
Blauer Portugieser

Baden

Germany's most southerly wine-producing region, Baden, enjoys a warm, sunny climate that sets it apart from other regions in the country. Situated in the south-west of Germany, neighbouring the French region of Alsace (pages 66–7), the region sits along the eastern bank of the Rhine River and is protected from extreme weather by the Rhine Rift, a valley that sits between the Vosges Mountains and the Black Forest. The south of the region is dominated by Lake Constance, and the grapes that grow around its banks are further warmed by the reflection of the light bouncing off its surface. The result of all this sunshine is that the region is known for rich, potent wines that are distinct from those produced in other regions of Germany.

The area is divided almost equally between red and white grapes, with Pinot Noir (sold as Spätburgunder) and Müller-Thurgau being the top varietal in each camp. Examples of Pinot Noir from Baden are notably full-bodied and rich in acidity, and have a finish reminiscent of the forest floor.

White wines from the region tend to be dry and earthy, with Müller-Thurgau being the most planted grape, though Grauburgunder (Pinot Gris) is becoming increasingly popular. Riesling, so popular in the rest of Germany because of how it performs in cooler climates, accounts for only a small portion of the grapes grown here.

Common varietals in Baden wines

White	Red
Müller-Thurgau	Spätburgunder
Grauburgunder	Pinot Meunier
Riesling	Regent

Franken

Situated along the Main River, the longest tributary of the Rhine, and to the east of Frankfurt, the region of Franken (also known as Franconia) can be loosely split into three sub-regions. Each of these has a unique landscape and specialises in a different style of wine.

If you're looking for red wine from Franken, look to Mainviereck. The sandstone soil and warm climate of this area, positioned in western Franken, is best suited for growing red wine grapes, and Spätburgunder and Frühburgunder dominate the vineyards here.

The Maindreieck region is known for its rocky soils in which white wine grapes such as Silvaner and Müller-Thurgau thrive. In fact, the area is known for producing some of the best wines from Silvaner grapes in the world. Although often overshadowed by other white grapes common to Germany, such as Riesling and Grüner Veltliner, Silvaner from this region possesses a clean minerality that is highly regarded and well worth seeking out.

The mountainous Steigerwald is Franken's third notable wine region and is also known for its white wines; the soil here is rich and the grapes are grown at the highest altitude of all Franken's vineyards. The wines produced in Stiegerwald are full-flavoured and rich in fruit, as opposed to the clean minerality of Maindreieck whites.

The wines of Franken are easy to identify due to the unique shape of the bottles used here. The *bocksbeutel* is a flat, rounded vessel that originated in the area and is largely unique to it, though similar bottles can be found in parts of Italy and Portugal. Though the bottle is distinctive, it can cause problems if you're planning on storing your wine in a traditional rack or wine fridge. That said, if you're shopping for Franken wines, it is well worth seeking out this bottle style, as only higher-quality wines are allowed to use it.

Common varietals in Franken wines

White
Silvaner
Müller-Thurgau

Red
Spätburgunder
Frühburgunder

Mittelrhein

The Mittelrhein (Middle Rhine) stretches for 75 miles along the banks of the Rhine River. The steep, south-facing slopes enjoy long hours of sun and are perfect for ripening the region's star grape, Riesling, which accounts for 65 per cent of Mittelrhein's output. As a whole, the region is dominated by white wine grapes, with 85 per cent of wine production being given over to white wines.

Outside of Germany, the region is better known for its dramatic landscapes and tourism opportunities than its wine, and even in the domestic market it is overshadowed by its more famous neighbours, such as the Mosel Valley and Rheingau. Another reason that wines from Mittelrhein haven't made an impact on the international market is that yields are low. The steep slopes surrounding the Rhine are hard to farm and not suited to high levels of output.

Rieslings from Mittelrhein are fruity, aromatic and perhaps a little sweeter than is fashionable, but there are some notable examples to be found, particularly those from the Boppard Hamm vineyard, which are well worth seeking out. Red wine in the region only accounts for a small amount of the total output, with the most common grape varietal being Spätburgunder (Pinot Noir).

Common varietals in Mittelrhein wines

White
Riesling
Müller-Thurgau
Kerner

Red
Spätburgunder
Dornfelder

Mosel Valley

The Mosel Valley is known the world over for producing world-class Riesling. Situated along the banks of the Mosel River and one of the northernmost wine regions in the world, the Mosel Valley has a cool climate, but the steep angle of the riverbanks on which the region's vineyards grow means that the grapes are able to absorb the full warmth of the sun throughout the day. The river plays a part in this too, reflecting the sun back onto the vines and helping to produce fruit that is beautifully fresh and gently ripe.

The area's soils are rich in slate, which imparts fragrant aromas and a clean mineral finish to the wines produced here. This is white wine country, with over 90 per cent of all wine produced in the valley being white, and over 60 per cent of it made from Riesling grapes. The Riesling here is regarded as some of the best in the world and can present as anything from very dry through to sweet, though generally German Rieslings tend to be sweeter and more aromatic than their French counterparts. Mosel Valley Rieslings can respond well to laying down for a few years and can open up to reveal more complex flavour notes.

The small amount of red wine in the region is largely made up of Spätburgunder, which is well worth trying if you are in the region, though possibly not worth seeking out otherwise.

Common varietals in Mosel Valley wines

White
Riesling
Müller-Thurgau
Elbling
Kerner

Red
Spätburgunder

Nahe

Another of Germany's wine regions that is mainly associated with white wines, Nahe is situated to the south-west of Frankfurt, along the banks of the river Nahe. Like many of Germany's white wine regions, Riesling is the key grape varietal here and accounts for around 30 per cent of the grapes grown.

The climate of the region is typified by generous sunshine, low rainfall and mild to cool temperatures. The stony soils store warmth from the sun that transfers to the vines in the cool evenings and the steep valleys of the region prevent frost from forming, protecting the grapes from being damaged.

The area is known for its geological diversity and there is a multitude of soil types to be found within the region, the most common being slate, limestone and volcanic. This spectrum of soil types means the wines produced here, such as Riesling, are produced in a variety of styles, from dry to sweet. Wines from the lower part of the region, for instance, are often richer and fuller-bodied than those produced in Upper Nahe.

Common varietals in Nahe wines

White
Riesling
Müller-Thurgau
Silvaner
Pinot Blanc

Red
Dornfelder
Spätburgunder

Pfalz

The second-largest winemaking area in Germany in terms of production, Pfalz or Palatinate, is one of the country's mildest regions, sharing a climate with the French region of Alsace, with which it shares a border. The vines grown in the region are positioned between the Haardt mountain range and the Palatinate Forest, both of which provide shelter from extreme weather and trap warm air, creating a mild microclimate in which grapes can thrive.

Both red and white wines from the region lean towards dry, full-bodied styles that can be richly aromatic. Despite Riesling being the most widely grown grape in the region and the majority of wine produced here being white, the area is actually one of Germany's biggest producers of red wine, with wonderful examples of Spätburgunder and Dornfelder being produced in the region.

Pfalz's Riesling wines are notable for being full-bodied and with reduced acidity compared to the famous Mosel Valley Rieslings that many are familiar with. Other mild and quaffable white wines from the region are made from Müller-Thurgau and Silvaner grapes.

Common varietals in Nahe wines

White
Riesling
Müller-Thurgau
Silvaner

Red
Dornfelder
Blauer Portugieser
Spätburgunder

Rheingau

One of Germany's most highly regarded wine regions, Rheingau is situated along the right bank of the Rhine in the shelter of the Taunus Mountains. Like much of Germany, the area is known for its Riesling, which accounts for almost 80 per cent of all growth in the region and has a pronounced minerality from the loose soil that is rich with chalk and gravel. The area is famous for its beautiful scenery and is home to some of Germany's oldest and most revered wine estates, making it an excellent base if planning a holiday to explore the wines of Germany.

The area is known for its mild winters and, as a result, grapes enjoy a long growing season and can be left on the vine until fully ripe. This leads to Rieslings that are noticeably more full-bodied than those produced in other areas.

After Riesling, the remainder of the wine output is largely made up of Spätburgunder, of which the area produces many high-quality examples that are notable for their silky texture and pronounced blackberry flavours.

Common varietals in Rheingau wines

White
Riesling

Red
Spätburgunder

Rheinhessen

Another region that specialises in white wine, Rheinhessen is notable for the fact that Riesling shares an equal footing with other, lesser-known grape varietals, with Müller-Thurgau being among the most commonly grown. Situated between Rheingau and Pfalz, the region runs along the western bank of the Rhine in an area that is known for its rolling hills, many of which are used as farmland.

The area spreads away from the river, but the grapes that are grown right along its banks are regarded as being of the highest quality and most reflective of the area's *terroir*. The Rhine itself plays a part here as its surface and surrounding valleys warm the grapes and aid the ripening process.

The area is famous for the production of the sweet wine Liebfraumilch, which was very popular in the UK in the 1950s but has now dropped out of fashion as tastes have changed. Liebfraumilch's legacy has been to damage the reputation of the area, which is still associated by some wine snobs with sweet, poor-quality wines. In fact, the majority of the white wines now produced are dry or off-dry.

Red wines from the region are led by the Dornfelder grape, which is designed to be drunk young in a similar fashion to Beaujolais Nouveau (see page 71).

Common varietals in Rheingau wines

White
Riesling
Müller-Thurgau
Silvaner

Red
Dornfelder
Spätburgunder

Italy

Wine is part of the fabric of Italian culture, with Italy being responsible for producing more wine on a yearly basis than any other country in the world. Search the supermarket shelves and mass-produced Italian Pinot Grigios and Proseccos will immediately jump out at you, and there can be a lot of joy to be found in these accessible, easy-drinking wines.

Scratch the surface of Italy, though, and you will find a country that makes some of the most refined and delicious wines in the world. From the rule-breaking and revolutionary Super Tuscans (see pages 8–9) to the classic Chiantis or refined Brunellos, Italian wines are highly regarded and sought after by wine enthusiasts all over the world.

Italy's wines are often labelled by appellation, so a little knowledge of the grapes grown in each region can be a huge help when choosing something to drink. In a similar way to the AOC system in France (see page 64) each appellation is granted a quality classification ranging from DOCG, the highest, to Vino da Tavola, the lowest, and these designations are clearly marked on any Italian wine label.

Italian Wine Classifications

Italian wine production is closely regulated and all wine produced in Italy falls into one of the four categories outlined below:

DOCG (Denominazione di Origine Controllata e Garantita)

This is the highest level of wine classification in Italy. It was created in the 1980s as a way of signifying truly exceptional Italian wines, as it was felt there was a wide variance in the quality of DOC wines, which had been the highest classification up to that point. DOCG appellations tend to be very small, focussed areas where the quality can be closely monitored and controlled. Wines from DOCG appellations tend to have the greatest expression of the *terroir* of any Italian wines and are made using the methods traditional to each region. For wine to achieve DOCG status, the wine must be made of the approved grapes for that appellation, the grapes must be grown there, and the wine made within the appellation itself. Crucially, and the thing that really separates DOCG wines from DOC wines, is that the wine must be tasted and approved by an official panel. There are 74 appellations that have been granted DOCG status in Italy.

DOC (Denominazione di Origine Controllata)

Much like DOCG wines, DOC wines must be made from an approved list of grapes for the area and the grapes must be grown and the wine bottled within that area. DOC appellations tend to be slightly larger than DOCGs, with 329 appellations currently being granted this designation. The main difference between DOCG and DOC wines is that DOC wines do not come with a guarantee (*garantita*) supplied by the Italian government in terms of taste testing the wines before they are put on sale.

IGT (Indicazione Geografica Tipica)

The next rung down the ladder for Italian wines actually contains some of its most exciting. IGT wines have to be made from grapes grown within the region, but what the grapes are and how the wine is made is not monitored. This can mean that IGT wines are lower quality than DOCG and DOC wines, but it also means that there are some wonderful examples of high-quality wine that are made in a way that does not conform to the traditional standards found in this category. Many of the Super Tuscans (see pages 8–9) fall into this category, as although they are made with great skill and care, they are produced from grapes that are not traditionally grown in Italy.

VDT (Vino da Tavola)

Wines designated as Vino da Tavola (table wine) can be made from grapes grown anywhere in Italy and, as such, have no expression of an area's *terroir*. They are generally lower quality and cheaper to buy than other Italian wines but are rarely exported outside of Italy.

Italian wine regions

Abruzzo

Positioned in southern central Italy, Abruzzo is known as Italy's greenest region, famous for its lush green parklands, imposing mountains and extensive Adriatic coastline to the east. This unique landscape with its long, hot summers combined with generous rainfall is ideal for growing grapes. Much of the wine made in the region is mass-produced and shipped out of Italy for consumption, with the USA and Germany being among the biggest consumers of Abruzzo wines. Though production in the region is high, the proportion of wine being made to DOC standards accounts for just 20 per cent of the region's output.

The region contains two designated DOCGs (see page 102), and seven DOC classifications, with perhaps the best-known wine being Montepulciano d'Abruzzo DOC, a rich tannic red which opens up nicely with a little aging.

The most notable white wine in the region is Trebbiano d'Abruzzo DOC, which is low in acidity, slightly floral on the nose, and often oaked and blended with Chardonnay to produce a wine rich with the flavour of orchard fruit and an underlying nuttiness.

Varietals in DOCG and DOC Abruzzo wines

White
Trebbiano
Pecorino
Passerina

Red
Montepulciano

Basilicata

Situated in the deep south of Italy, the small wine-producing region of Basilicata is known for its independent producers who make low yields of very high-quality wine. The now extinct Monte Vulture volcano is responsible for the region's rich volcanic soil, on which grapes thrive. This, combined with long, hot summers and refreshing breezes from the Ionian Sea, makes for ideal growing conditions.

The region is home to four DOCs and a single DOCG, which are responsible for just a small fraction of the wine produced in the region, with most Basilicata wines being designated as either IGT or Vino da Tavola (see page 103).

The region's one DOCG appellation is Aglianico del Vulture Superiore. The 'Superiore' is a signifier that this wine contains a slightly higher than average minimum alcohol content of 13.5%. Made with thick-skinned Aglianico del Vulture grapes grown in the volcanic soil around Monte Vulture, the young wines of this appellation are full-bodied, acidic and tannic, but with a little aging become much softer and more rounded on the palate.

Varietals in DOCG and DOC Basilicata wines

White
Malvasia Bianca di Basilicata
Greco

Red
Aglianico del Vulture
Sangiovese
Cabernet Sauvignon
Malvasia Nera di Basilicata

Campania

Naples, Capri, Positano and the Amalfi Coast – Campania is doubtless one of the most beautiful and storied regions of Italy. Situated in south-west Italy along the Mediterranean coast, the region enjoys long, hot summers with refreshing sea breezes. The soil here is rich in minerals due to the presence of the still active Mount Vesuvius, which last erupted in 1944.

There are four appellations with DOCG status and 10 with DOC status in the region, which produce white, red, rosé and sparkling wines, though Campania is best known for its reds. Of all the region's wines, Taurasi DOCG, made from Aglianico grapes, is perhaps the best-regarded and is often named as a more affordable alternative to the Brunellos of Piedmont and Barolos of Tuscany. For white wines look to Greco di Tufo DOCG or Fiano di Avellino DOCG, which both hail from the province of Irpinia.

Common varietals in DOCG and DOC Campania wines

The region is home to over 100 native grapes, but the list below covers the most important:

White
Falanghina
Fiano
Greco

Red
Aglianico
Piedirosso
Sciascinoso

Emilia-Romagna

This large region in northern Italy – spanning almost the entire width of the country and home to the city of Bologna – is synonymous with Italian cuisine, with Parmesan cheese, balsamic vinegar and spaghetti Bolognese all hailing from the area. Wine from the region deserves just as much attention.

Including 20 DOC designated appellations and a single DOCG, there are many quality wines to be found in the area. Romagna Albana DOCG produces a still white wine primarily made from Albana grapes. The wines are produced in either *bianco*, *passito* or *reserve passito* style, ranging from dry to sweet.

Perhaps the most famous wine from the region is Lambrusco, made from a red grape of the same name. The most notable Lambrusco appellations are Lambrusco Reggiano DOC, Lambrusco Grasparossa di Castelvetro DOC, Lambrusco di Sorbara DOC and Lambrusco Salamino di Santa Croce DOC. Though Lambrusco wines are often thought of as sweet, and many are, *secco* (dry) and *semisecco* (off-dry) varieties are available.

Common varietals in DOCG and DOC Emilia-Romagna wines

White
Pignoletto
Albana
Malvasia
Trebbiano

Red
Lambrusco
Centesimino
Sangiovese

Friuli–Venezia Giulia

This region to the far north-east of Italy, sharing borders with Austria to the north and Slovenia to the east, is home to some of Italy's finest white wines, with Prosecco and Pinot Grigio being the star players. There are 10 designated DOC appellations in the area and four DOCGs.

Friuli Grave DOC is one of the best known in the region and responsible for producing notably superior varieties of Pinot Grigio. The area's gravelly soil imparts a refined minimalistic quality to the wines produced here.

Perhaps the second-most famous sparkling wine in the world after Champagne, Prosecco can only come from nine DOC and DOCG regions in north-east Italy spanning Friuli-Venezia Giulia and neighbouring Veneto. Prosecco is made from at least 85 per cent Glera grapes (also known as Prosecco), with the remaining volume often being made up of Chardonnay or Pinot Grigio. When buying Prosecco, make sure that you look for either a DOC or DOCG classification on the bottle. The reason that Prosecco is so affordable in comparison to Champagne is down to the production method, with Prosecco using the *Charmat* method rather than the *méthode traditionnelle* used to make Champagne. Rather than fermenting wines for a second time in the bottle to create the signature bubbles, wines made using the *Charmat* method receive their second fermentation in large steel tanks, which is both quicker and lower in labour than the *méthode traditionnelle*. Wines made in this way tend to have a more pronounced fruit flavour and are more lightly carbonated than those made using the *méthode traditionnelle*.

Common varietals in DOCG and DOC Friuli-Venezia Giulia wines

White
Friulano
Pinot Grigio
Sauvignon Blanc
Pinot Bianco
Chardonnay
Glera (Prosecco)

Red
Lambrusco
Merlot
Cabernet Franc
Cabernet Sauvignon
Carménère

Le Marche

Found between the Adriatic Sea to the east and the Apennine mountain range to the west, Le Marche (pronounced 'Le Mar-Kay') is positioned in the central-east region of Italy. The region's vineyards are found inland on the hills and lower slopes of the Apennine Mountains where the soil is rich with limestone and clay, on which the vines thrive.

There are five DOCG and 15 DOC appellations in the region, though only a handful of these have made a real mark outside of Italy. The region is best known for its white wines, with Verdicchio being the region's, and one of Italy's, highest regarded dry whites. Verdicchio is notable for being one of the few whites that can benefit from aging, due to its ability to express complex flavours. These can be jarring when the wine is drunk young, but can achieve balance and harmony when laid down for a few years. The *verdi* in Verdicchio is derived from the Italian word for green, and these wines have a yellowy-green hue that makes them easy to identify. Good examples of the wine are crisp and acidic, with notes of citrus and a slightly creamy, bitter finish reminiscent of almonds. Verdicchio also makes lovely sparkling wine under the name Verdicchio Spumante, which is well worth seeking out.

Notable red wines from the region tend to be made from either Montepulciano or Sangiovese grapes. Good examples include those from Rosso Conero DOCG, which produces rich, inky reds with herbal aromas and notes of cherry.

Common varietals in DOCG and DOC Le Marche wines

White	Red
Verdicchio	Lacrima
Pecorino	Vernaccia Nera
Passerina	Montepulciano
Biancame	Sangiovese
Trebbiano	

Liguria

Situated in north-west Italy and bordering France, Liguria is famous for being home to the beautiful Italian Riviera, which carves a dramatic path along the coast of the Mediterranean sea. The area is best known for its white wines, with the Vermentino grape being dominant in the wines produced here. It's a small region with only eight DOC appellations and no DOCG designations.

The climate here is unsurprisingly Mediterranean, and the grapes are grown in stony soils clinging to the steep cliffs that follow the dramatic coastline. The vineyards provide a secondary purpose along these craggy ledges in that the roots of the vines cling to the sides of the cliffs and prevent landslides and erosion. Because the vineyards are situated on such steep inclines, the grapes are generally harvested by hand by small producers.

Notable appellations include Cinque Terre DOC, which produces straw-coloured whites that are dry on the palate with a soft, floral aroma. Though Vermentino is king here, Cinque Terre wines are made with at least 40 per cent Bosco, with the remainder being made up of Albarola or Vermentino.

When it comes to red wines, perhaps the region's most distinctive examples can be found to the west of Liguria, close to the French border, in Rossese di Dolceacqua DOC. The Rossese grape thrives at high altitudes, so the alpine valleys of the French-Italian border provide ideal growing conditions for the grape, which produces a red wine with high acidity and perfumed herbal notes that are pleasantly bitter on the finish.

Common varietals in DOC Liguria wines

White	Red	
Albarola	Dolcetto	Sangiovese
Vermentino (Pigato)	Grenache	Ciliegiolo
Bosco	Pollerra Nera	
Lumassina	Rossese	

Lombardy

Situated in central northern Italy, along the border of Switzerland, Lombardy is known for its stunning lakes, the region's capital city of Milan, and its high proportion of UNESCO World Heritage sites. Though it's one of the largest and most populous regions of Italy, it produces a relatively small amount of wine, albeit in a lot of different styles. There are five DOCG and twenty DOC appellations in the region, and many native and non-native grape varietals.

The region is perhaps best known for being the only area outside of Piedmont (page 114–15) to specialise in the Nebbiolo grape, known in Lombardy as Chiavennasca, which thrives in the alpine valleys of the Valtellina subregion along the Swiss–Italian border. These wines are produced in two of the regions DOCG appellations, Valtellina Superiore DOCG and Sforzato di Valtellina DOCG, and are well worth seeking out for any fans of their more famous Piedmontese cousins Barolo and Barbaresco.

The sparkling wine of Lombardy deserves special note for being Italy's finest, despite the fact that it is relatively unknown. Franciacorta DOCG produces fizz using the *méthode traditionnelle* (see page 5) and can fetch prices similar to French Champagne as a result. The wines are made from a combination of Chardonnay, Pinot Noir and Pinot Blanc, and are highly prized and worth seeking out as a delicious alternative to Champagne that is sure to be a talking point.

The region isn't that well known for its still whites, but for good examples look to Lugana DOC, which produces dry whites with good acidity and notes of citrus from Trebbiano grapes.

Common varietals in DOCG and DOC Lombardy wines

White
Chardonnay
Moscato
Pinot Bianco
Pinot Grigio
Riesling
Trebbiano
Welschriesling

Red
Barbera
Bonarda
Cabernet Sauvignon
Carménère
Croatina
Groppello
Lambrusco
Marzemino
Merlot
Moscato Nero
Nebbiolo
Pinot Nero
Uva Rara

Piedmont

One of the most storied of all of Italy's wine-producing regions, Piedmont is famous the world over for its intense, tannic reds Barolo and Barbaresco, which are made from Nebbiolo.

Located in the north of Italy, Piedmont shares borders with both France and Switzerland. The landscape of high mountains and low valleys creates a unique climate that is prized for growing Nebbiolo grapes.

These famous wines are celebrated for their high acidity, fresh berry and floral aromas and spicy notes. They also age brilliantly, becoming smooth and silky over time, and are best drunk aged 10 years and over, when they can fetch very high prices. In terms of taste, the difference between Barolo and Barbaresco is that Barolo is more tannic and is aged for longer before being sold. The cause of these tannins is the soil that the grapes are grown in. Nebbiolo from Barolo DOCG is grown in soil that is lower in nutrients than Barbaresco, which means it takes longer to ripen and spends longer on the vine as a result. This extended ripening period results in thicker-skinned grapes, which is the source of the heightened tannins in Barolo.

Despite the popularity of these Nebbiolo-made wines, they actually account for a relatively small proportion of wines produced in the area, with the most widely grown red grape actually being Barbera. Barbera is grown throughout Piedmont and used to make many good-quality reds with heft and flavour, though the world's enthusiasm for Barolo does somewhat overshadow them.

When it comes to white wine, Piedmont is famous for producing crisp whites, such as Cortese di Gavi DOCG (sometimes labelled as Gavi di Gavi), from 100 per cent Cortese grapes. The region is also known for sparkling wines, in particular Asti Spumante DOCG, made from the highly perfumed Moscato Bianco grape. Though once in high demand, the last few decades have seen a decline in the popularity of Asti wines as consumers' tastes have veered away from sweeter styles of sparkling wine towards varieties with a dryer finish.

Common varietals in DOCG and DOC Piedmont wines

White
Cortese
Arneis
Moscato
Chardonnay

Red
Nebbiolo
Barbera
Dolcetto

Puglia

Situated in the far south-east of Italy, forming the heel of Italy's boot, Puglia is known for its long, hot summers, miles upon miles of beautiful coastline and the production of some of the world's finest olive oil. The wine here is not to be missed either, and Puglian wine can be reliably delicious and good value. The region contains four DOCG and twenty-nine DOC appellations.

Historically, Puglian wine was used to blend and boost wines of other Italian regions, but as respect for New World wines began to increase and grapes grown in hot climates began to be recognised for their ability to produce world-class wines, Puglian wines in turn were recognised in their own right.

The region is best known for its robust, full-flavoured reds, with the Primitivo grape (known elsewhere as Zinfandel) being the star player, and prized for its early ripening. The best examples include the Primitivo di Manduria Dolce Naturale DOCG and the non-sweet Primitivo di Manduria DOC.

When it comes to white wine, growth is dominated by Verdeca and Fiano grapes. Verdeca produces a clean-tasting wine with herbal notes – good examples can be found in Locorotondo DOC and Martina Franca DOC. Fiano produces a more floral wine, with notes of tropical fruit and vanilla.

Common varietals in DOCG and DOC Puglia wines

White
Verdeca
Fiano

Red
Primitivo
Negroamaro

Sardinia

The second-largest of Italy's islands after Sicily, Sardinia sits over 100 miles to the west of mainland Italy and has a unique climate and landscape that sets it apart from other Italian regions. Unlike other areas of Italy, the wines of Sardinia are mostly labelled by varietal rather than appellation. This is because the island was under Spanish rule for much of its early winemaking history, which also plays a part when looking at the grape varietals that are grown here. Sardinia has one DOCG and fifteen DOC appellations.

When it comes to red wine, Sardinia's signature grape is Cannonau (known as Grenache in France), which produces a robust wine that is low in acidity and has notes of autumn fruits and tobacco. Famously, this wine has been linked to the long lifespans of the Sardinian population, with many believing that, drunk in moderation, it has antioxidant properties that are linked to heart health.

Sardinia's most commonly found white wine is made from the region's Vermentino grapes, which produces refreshingly acidic wine with crisp apple notes. Great examples can be found in the island's only DOCG appellation, Vermentino di Gallura DOCG, which is located in the north-east of Sardinia.

Common varietals in DOCG and DOC Sardinian wines

White	Red
Vermentino	Cannonau (Grenache)
Nuragus	Monica
Nasco	Carignano
Moscato	Barbera Sarda
Chardonnay	

Sicily

Italy's largest winemaking region, the island of Sicily is situated off the south-west coast of the mainland and dominated by the mighty Mount Etna, one of the world's most active volcanos. Sicily is home to twenty-three DOC and just one DOCG appellations, with a single overriding DOC (Sicilia DOC) covering the whole island.

The island's red wines are dominated by Nero d'Avola grapes, which thrive in the island's volcanic soil. Nero d'Avola is used to produce wines that range from clean and easy drinking to full-bodied and tannic, depending on where on the island the grapes are grown. Look to Sicily's single DOCG appellation, Cerasuolo di Vittoria DOCG, for full-bodied varieties that are rich with the flavours of ripe autumn fruit with a background of spice and tobacco. Other notable red wines to look out for include those from Etna DOC, where Nerello grapes grow on the slopes of Mount Etna. These wines have been compared to the Barolos of Piedmont so are a good alternative if you're a fan of Barolo and are looking to try something new.

White wine production in Sicily is dominated by Marsala, a world-famous fortified wine made from the white grapes Catarratto, Grillo and Inzolia. Marsala is made by adding fortified grape to wine and leaving it to age for several years. The resulting wine is sweet and nutty with a deep caramel hue. Red varieties of Marsala wines are also available, though not as widely as the white.

Common varietals in DOCG and DOC Sicilian wines

White	Red
Catarratto	Nero D'Avola
Grillo	Nerello
Inzolia	Frappato
Carricante	

Trentino-Alto Adige

Situated in the far north of Italy and sharing a border with Austria and Switzerland, Trentino-Alto Adige is a region dominated by two mountain ranges, the Dolomites and the Alps. The area has strong Austrian and Germanic influences and only became part of Italy in 1919. These influences are evident in the grapes grown in the region, with German varietals such as Gewürztraminer having a strong foothold here. Despite being a relatively small player in the world of Italian wines, proportionally Trentino-Alto Adige has a higher percentage of DOC appellations than any other region, with 98 per cent of wine produced within the region being granted DOC status.

The vineyards here cling to the mountainous slopes and valleys and are warmed by air that rises from the valley floors on sunny days. White wine in the area makes up about 60 per cent of all production, and there are world-class crisp Pinot Grigios to be found in the area. For good-quality examples look to Trentino DOC, which is also renowned for its excellent sparkling wines.

The area is lesser known for its reds, but there are some really interesting examples to be found. Red wine grapes here tend to be either Schiava, used for producing an aromatic, lighter-bodied red reminiscent of Pinot Noir, or Lagrein, used to produce a fuller-bodied wine high in acid and tannins with a mineralistic undertone.

Common varietals in DOC Trentino-Alto Adige wines

White	Red
Pinot Grigio	Schiava
Gewürztraminer	Lagrein
Chardonnay	Pinot Noir
	Refosco

Tuscany

Of all of Italy's wine regions, Tuscany is perhaps the most celebrated, and rightly so. Situated in north central Italy with a coastline to the Tyrrhenian Sea, the area has a varying landscape which is home to 11 DOCG and 41 DOC appellations.

Traditionally, much of the red wine made here is from Sangiovese grapes. The area is home to many household names in the world of red wine, all made with Sangiovese: Brunello, Chianti and Montepulciano all find their home here. In more recent years, the cult of the Super Tuscan has taken hold, with producers experimenting with non-native grapes, such as Cabernet Sauvignon and Cabernet Franc. Perhaps the most famous of these Super Tuscans is Sassicaia (see pages 8–9), which was the first of the Super Tuscans to be awarded its own DOC, thus legitimising its use of non-native grapes and winemaking techniques.

While Tuscany is primarily a red wine region, it is also famous for its white dessert wine, Vin Santo, which is made from Trebbiano and Malvasia grapes that are slowly dried after harvesting to concentrate the natural sugars in the fruit. These wines are aged in chestnut barrels for anything from three to ten years, and the finished products are highly prized.

Common varietals in DOCG and DOC Tuscan wines

White
Trebbiano
Malvasia

Red
Sangiovese
Cabernet Sauvignon
Cabernet Franc
Merlot
Pinot Noir
Syrah

Umbria

Situated in central Italy, Umbria is notable for being the only Italian winemaking region that contains neither a coastline nor a border with another country. The region is dominated by the Apennine mountain range to the east, along its border with Le Marche, and the wide valley of the Tiber River to the west, around which most of Umbria's vineyards can be found. The area contains two DOCG and thirteen DOC appellations.

Though perhaps best known for its white wines, Umbria's two DOCG appellations are actually for red wine. Montefalco Sagrantino DOCG makes wines from 100 per cent Sagrantino grapes in two styles, *secco* (dry) and *passito* (sweet). Sagrantino grapes are very thick-skinned and both styles of wine are high in tannins, have impressive heft and body and require significant aging before being suitable for drinking.

The second DOCG appellation is Torgiano Rosso Riserva DOCG, which produces reds constructed of at least 70 per cent Sangiovese, with the remainder being made up of Cabernet Sauvignon, Merlot, Canaiolo or Colorino. These wines are notable for their bright ruby-red colouration and delicate floral bouquet and benefit from aging for up to a decade before drinking.

Umbria's white wines comprise the bulk of the region's output, with Trebbiano and Grechetto being the key grape varietals grown here. The most notable whites of the region are those produced in Orvieto DOC, which are a blend of the two grapes and are notable for their delicate citrus flavours. These wines range from dry (*secco*) to off-sweet (*amabile*), depending on how long the grapes have been left on the vine to intensify their natural sugars.

Common varietals in DOCG and DOC Umbria wines

White
Trebbiano
Grechetto
Chardonnay

Red
Sagrantino
Sangiovese
Sauvignon
Cabernet
Merlot
Pinot Noir

Veneto

Located in the north-east of Italy, Veneto is Italy's largest wine producer by volume, producing around 20 per cent of all of Italy's DOC wines.

The most important white grape in the area is Garganega, which is used to make the region's famous Soave wines. A subtle wine with a floral nose and notes of soft summer fruits. Soave wines must be at least 70 per cent Garganega, with the remaining often made up of Trebbiano grapes.

Along with Friuli-Venezia Giulia, Veneto is responsible for much of the production of Italy's glut of Prosecco (see page 108), which the world can't seem to get enough of. These wines are made from at least 85 per cent Glera grapes, with the remainder being made up of Chardonnay or Pinot Noir. Quality can vary, so it is best to look to the region's two DOCG appellations for Prosecco, Conegliano-Valdobbiadene Prosecco Superiore DOCG and Asolo Prosecco Superiore DOCG.

For red wines, look to the region's famous Valpolicella wines, which are made in a variety of different styles, mostly from the Veneto's native Corvina grapes. Valpolicella DOC and Valpolicella Ripasso DOC produce fruity, easy-drinking reds, though the Ripasso varieties have a bit more heft. Valpolicella wines that are labelled as Amarone della Valpolicella DOCG are perhaps the most special and are made with grapes that have been partially dried to concentrate their flavour. The resulting wine is dry, full of flavour and high in alcohol at around 17% ABV.

Common varietals in DOCG and DOC Veneto wines

White	Red
Garganega	Corvina
Trebbiano	Rondinella
Glera	Molinara

Portugal

Ranking 11th in the world in terms of production, Portugal holds a relatively small space on the international wine stage, with its world-famous fortified port wines (see pages 130-1) being the country's most renowned export.

There's so much more to Portugal than port, though, and the varied climate and topography of the country make for a vibrant and interesting wine industry. With its long Atlantic coast, lush valleys and flinty mountain ranges, Portugal offers a thriving wine culture, with over 250 regional varietals to discover. Vinho Verde, hailing from the Minho region in the north-west of the country (see page 133) is of particular note for its slight effervescence, crisp acidity and floral aroma.

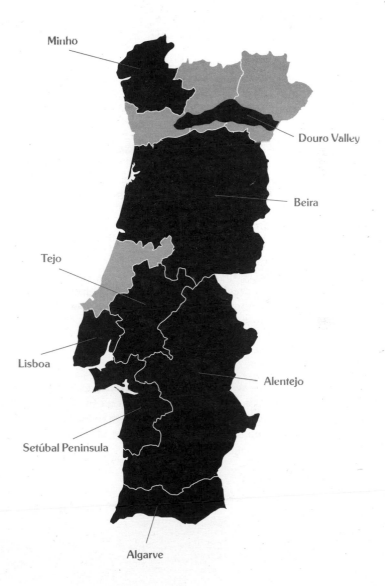

Minho

Douro Valley

Beira

Tejo

Lisboa

Alentejo

Setúbal Peninsula

Algarve

Portuguese Wine Classifications

Like other EU countries, Portugal operates a three-tier classification system for its wine appellations. From top to bottom, these classifications are:

Denominação de Origem Controlada (DOC)
There are currently just over 30 DOC appellations in Portugal. This tier represents wines that are produced in a specific geographical area. DOC areas are governed by strict rules relating to the permitted varietals and yields as well as production techniques used for making the wine.

Vinho Regional (IPG)
These are wines that are also produced in a designated area but are subject to less stringent rules around grape varietals and production techniques.

Vinho
These wines are table wines mostly made for local consumption. As such, they will rarely be seen outside of Portugal. The grapes can come from anywhere in Portugal and there are very few rules in terms of yield or production.

Portuguese wine regions

Alentejo

This large region in the south of Portugal is known for its red blends, rich with soft fruit flavours and mellow tannins. The region contains a single DOC, also called Alentejo (though not all Alentejo wines are included within the DOC). For the best red examples look to the wines of Borba, Evora and Redondo, where local vineyards are dominated by red Aragonês (Tempranillo), Abundante (Grenache) and Alfrocheiro grapes.

White wines from the region are aromatic and reflective of the long hours of sun that Alentejo enjoys. Local varietals, such as Antao Vaz, produce wines that are high in alcohol and rich with tropical fruit flavours.

Common varietals in Alentejo DOC wines

White
Antao Vaz
Arinto
Chardonnay

Red
Aragonês
Abundante
Alfrocheiro Preto
Carignan
Baga

Algarve

Better known as a holiday destination than an area rich in wine production, the sun-baked soil of the Algarve may not seem like the natural place for a thriving wine industry. There are some gems to be found here, though, particularly within the region's only DOC of Lagos, which specialises in red varietals that thrive in dry climates, such as Castelão, Negra Mole and Trincadeira. These grapes are used to produce soft, supple red wines that are rich with the flavour of red fruits.

The region is less suited to growing white varietals, though it is possible to find pleasant examples of full-bodied aromatic whites made from Arinto and Malvasia Fina grapes.

Common varietals in Algarve DOC wines

White
Arinto
Malvasia Fina

Red
Castelão
Negra Mole
Trincadeira
Periquita

Beira

Situated in northern Portugal, Beira is a large wine region that contains several DOC appellations that are among the most highly regarded in the country. Among these is Dão DOC, which is situated along the length of the Dão River and is sheltered by two mountain ranges, both of which bring granite-rich soils to the area. Wines from Dão vary from rich, heavily tannic reds that are traditionally aged in oak, to fresh and fruity whites made from the native Encruzado grape.

Another notable DOC is Bairrada, situated close to the Atlantic coast, which brings cool breezes and high rainfall. The region is known for its sparkling white wines, which have a lively acidity and are made from a range of varietals including Baga, Arinto, Bical and Chardonnay.

Common varietals in Beira DOC wines

White
Arinto
Borrado das Moscas
Sercial
Fernão Pires
Malvasia

Red
Baga
Bastardo
Jaen
Marufo
Periquita

Douro Valley

Home to Portugal's world-famous port, the Douro Valley is one of the world's oldest wine regions. Port makes up around 50 per cent of wine produced in the region, with the rest being red and white wines made from a wide range of regional grapes, though these are not nearly as highly regarded.

Port is a wine that has been fortified with brandy to increase the ABV and aid in the prolonged aging that the wine is famous for. In its most common form, port is sweet and red, though there are many different styles available, including dry examples and those made with white grapes.

Port wines are produced with grapes grown in the Douro Valley, but this style of wine is also closely linked with the city of Porto, around 40 kilometres away, after which the wine is named, as this is where the wine was exported from historically.

Vineyards in the region are grown on stepped vineyards surrounding the banks of the Douro River, where the grapes receive the maximum amount of sun. These long hours of sunshine intensify the grapes' sweetness, making them perfect for vinification into port.

The production of port involves a very short fermentation process of just 24–36 hours, during which the maximum amount of flavour is extracted from the grape skins and must. Traditional foot treading still happens, though it is becoming more common to find mechanised alternatives. After the wine is fermented, it is fortified with a distilled grape brandy to raise the ABV to around 22%. The port is then aged in various sizes of neutral oak barrels or stainless steel tanks. Ports that are aged in larger barrels are exposed to less oxygen and are known as ruby ports; those that are aged in smaller barrels, and thus have greater exposure to oxygen, are known as tawny ports.

The names ruby and tawny are taken from the colour of the respective ports, with ruby port being a deep gemstone red, and tawny presenting with tinges of rusty golden brown. In flavour, ruby ports are sweeter and more fruit-forward, whereas tawny port has a more nutty, caramelised flavour that, while still sweet, benefits from being served cold.

Common varietals in Doura Valley wines

White
Gouveia
Malvasia Fina

Red
Touriga Nacional
Touriga Franca
Tinta Roriz (Tempranillo)
Tinta Borraçal
Tinta Câo

Lisboa

This small geographical region located on the Atlantic coast is actually Portugal's largest wine-producing region, by volume. Within its boundaries are nine DOC appellations specialising in a variety of wine styles.

The region's Serra de Montejunto hills and their surroundings protect the grapes from the cool breezes blowing in from the Atlantic Ocean, creating a temperate climate that is ideal for growing a range of varietals.

Among the most notable sub-regions is Bucelas DOC, known for its white wines made from Arinto grapes, which produce uniquely acidic wines for grapes grown in such a warm region. Colares DOC, notable for some of the oldest grapevines in Europe, produces highly astringent reds with a deep ruby colour. The region's best-regarded reds come from the DOC region on Alenquer, which produces hearty wines with notes of spice and black pepper.

There are some wonderful wines available in the region, and wines from Lisboa tend to be very affordable and offer a lot of bang for their buck.

Common varietals in Lisboa DOC wines

White	Red
Antao Vaz	Alfrocheiro Preto
Arinto	Baga
Borrado das Moscas	Bastardo
Chardonnay	Cabernet Sauvignon
Sercial	Graciano
Fernão Pires	Periquita

Minho

Home to the world-famous Vinho Verde, Minho is Portugal's most northerly wine region. Minho's only DOC is Vinho Verde itself, which enjoys a lush green landscape fed by long hours of sunshine, cool Atlantic breezes and relatively high rainfall.

Translating to 'green wine', Vinho Verde is bottled and released for sale just months after the region's grapes are harvested. The grapes themselves are grown on vines that are trained along high pergolas that allow wine producers with limited space to increase their yields. The slight fizz that distinguishes Vinho Verde wines was originally the result of malolactic conversion within the bottle and was seen as a mistake to be rectified, but it soon became synonymous with Vinho Verde wines and popular among its drinkers. Today, the wine is often slightly carbonated before bottling to emulate and control this natural effect.

Red and rosé Vinho Verde wines are available but these can be hard to source outside of the region itself. The white wines reign supreme, and good examples can be deeply refreshing when enjoyed heavily chilled on a hot summer's day.

Common varietals in Minho DOC wines

White	Red
Alvarinho	Azal Tinto
Arinto	Barroca
Avesso	Espadeiro
Azal	Rabo de Ovelha
Batoca	Vinhao
Loureiro	
Trajadura	

Setúbal Peninsula

Known for its fortified wine made from the Muscat grape, the Setúbal Peninsula is situated on the Atlantic coast just south of Lisbon. The area contains two DOCs, making different styles of wine.

Palmela DOC is known primarily as a red wine region, with a proliferation of Castelão grapes which thrive in the area's sandy soil. These wines are rich with aniseed and cherry and are often blended with international grapes, such as Cabernet Sauvignon and Syrah, to achieve beautifully balanced results.

The region's signature wine, Moscatel de Setúbal, comes from Setúbal DOC and is distinctive from other fortified wines for its highly floral aromas. These are achieved by adding the grape skins back into the fortified wine and allowing the flavours to develop for at least six months. In truth, Moscatel can be divisive and has not hit the popularity on the international market of Portugal's other famous fortified wine, port.

Common varietals in Setúbal Peninsula DOC wines

White
Muscat
Arinto
Chardonnay

Red
Castelão
Tempranillo
Syrah
Cabernet Sauvignon

Tejo

A landlocked region in central Portugal, Tejo is home to a climate eased by the influence of the Tagus River, which wends its way through the landscape. The area contains six DOC appellations that are known primarily for their red wine grapes, which thrive in the alluvial soils along the bank of the Tagus.

In recent years, native varietals have given way to international grapes, such as Cabernet Sauvignon and Chardonnay, as the area seeks to make its mark on the international wine scene. The area has come under scrutiny for its high yields and supposed focus on quantity over quality, though high-quality wines are available if you know where to look. In particular, look for wines from the sub-region of Bairro, whose vines are grown at cooler, higher elevations than much of the region, with vines that dig deep into the soil to produce fruit with a pronounced minerality. Other regions of note include Charneca, which produces bold, fruit-forward wines with a complex structure.

Common varietals in Tejo DOC wines

White
Arinto
Chardonnay
Sercial
Fernão Pires
Sauvignon Blanc

Red
Cabernet Sauvignon
Carignan
Merlot
Perquita
Pinot Noir

Spain

Spain is the second-largest wine producer in the world (after Italy), though much of its yield is used for producing another famous Spanish export: brandy. A country of numerous climates and landscapes, Spain produces a large number of signature wines in a variety of styles.

Known for its sun-baked plateaus, flinty mountainous regions and cooler coasts, which edge both the Mediterranean Sea and the Atlantic Ocean, it's no wonder that Spain has such variety on offer when it comes to wine. There are upwards of 600 grape varietals grown in the country, though the majority of the wine is produced from around 20 main varietals. A quarter of all Spanish grapes are Airén, which is primarily vinified into brandy but is sometimes blended with other white grapes to help balance a wine. For red wines, the most planted grape is Tempranillo, used to make the world-famous Rioja wines, which are among Spain's most famous exports.

Spain is also known for wonderful sparkling wines that offer an affordable, high-quality alternative to Champagne. Spanish Cava is made using the same method as Champagne (see page 5) and present with a similar lean quality that develops into a creamy nuttiness as the wines age.

Sherry, the fortified wine from around the city of Jerez in Andalucia (see pages 140–1), is another unique Spanish product that is sought out around the world. Once regarded as slightly outdated, in recent years sherry has gained a renewed popularity, finding a younger audience who are eager to explore its different styles and what they have to offer.

Galicia

Rioja

Navarra

Aragon

Castilla y León

Catalunya

Valencia

Murcia

Madrid

Andalucia

Spanish Wine Classifications

The Spanish wine classification system runs on a tiered scale similar to those used in other other European countries, though it includes some subcategories that are unique to Spanish wines. Running from highest to lowest, the tiers are:

Denominación de Origen Protegida (DOP)

This is the benchmark classification for high-quality Spanish wine and includes several specialist subcategories. DOP appellations are governed by strict rules regarding the permitted grape types, maximum yields and ABV percentages for the region's wines. There are around 100 DOP appellations in Spain. The two most significant subcategories of the DOP classification are:

Denominación de Origen Calificada (DOCa)

This classification is for wine appellations that have achieved consistent high-quality wines for a period of more than 10 years. There are only two DOCa appellations in Spain: Rioja and Priorat. The appellation of Ribera del Duero was granted permission to use the DOCa classification in 2008 but opted to remain classed as a standard DOP. The standard of Ribera del Duero wines is very high, though, so it is worth remembering that the area is worthy of DOCa status, even if it chooses not to use it.

Vinos de Pago (VdP)

This classification homes in on individual wine estates or vineyards that demonstrate exceptional quality. These classifications are generally used to indicate great-quality wine made in an area that isn't otherwise known for it. Most VdP wines will sit in an appellation that is otherwise not granted DOP status. There are around 19 VdP classified wine estates in Spain.

Vino de Calidad con Indicación Geográfica (VCIG)

This small category is a halfway house between DOP wines and those in lower categories. Wines made in this category are made to a higher quality than VdT wines (below) but fall short of full DOP status in some way.

Vino de la Tierra (VdT)

Translating to 'wine of the land', VdT wines are the middle tier of Spanish winemaking. Wines in this category are tied to grapes that are grown and vinified in a specific geographical area. There is no regulation over what type of grapes are used. There are around 50 designated VdTs in the country but, crucially, many areas are not covered by a VdT classification – wines made outside of VdT areas that do not qualify for DOP status will immediately be downgraded to Vino de Mesa (table wine). These wines are also known as IGP (Indicación Geográfica Protegida).

Vino de Mesa

This is the lowest tier of Spanish wines and there are relatively few rules around its production. The grapes can be grown anywhere in Spain or even in the EU. Though these wines are generally lower quality than the higher tiers of Spanish wine, there are some exceptions where skilled winemakers want to experiment with grapes from outside of the approved list of varietals at higher levels. These wines are generally made for consumption within Spain, though some examples can be found on the shelves of international supermarkets. It can be hard to tell the difference between a true table wine and one of a higher quality, but price can be a good indicator.

Spanish wine regions

Andalucia

Spain's southernmost winemaking region is famous around the world for its sherry, a fortified wine that finds its home around the city of Jerez. Situated close to Africa at the southern tip of Spain, Andalucia is known for its dramatic coastline and is the only European region which edges both the Atlantic and the Mediterranean.

Andalucia has seven DOP appellations, but easily the most famous is Jerez-Xérès-Sherry, which is formed in the triangle between the three towns of Jerez de la Frontera, El Puerto de Santa Maria and Sanlúcar de Barrameda.

Sherry is produced from three white grapes, with different grapes being used in different styles of sherry. Palomino, the dominant grape in Jerez-Xérès-Sherry DOP (accounting for over 90 per cent of grapes grown) is used to produce dry or *Fino* sherry. The other white grapes are Pedro Ximénez (PX), which produces a highly regarded sweet sherry, and Moscatel, which is also vinified into sweet sherry, though is less common than Pedro Ximénez.

Depending on the style of sherry, there are different processes involved in the production, but many styles of sherry are notable for the presence of *flor*, a layer of yeast that forms over the wine during fermentation and protects it from oxidization. The presence of *flor* allows for the wine to ferment for a longer period, normally around seven years. The wines are then fortified to around 15–17% ABV, after which they are barrel-aged and blended for the best end results.

Common varietals in Andalucian DOP wines

White
Palermo
Pedro Ximénez
Moscatel

Aragon

Located in the north-east of Spain, Aragon is one of the country's coolest wine-producing regions, with the high altitudes of the Pyrenees Mountains bringing lower temperatures that provide grapes with a longer growing season. The area's rocky soils infuse the grapes with a pronounced minerality.

The region is highly regarded for producing powerfully aromatic Garnacha wines, in both red and white varieties, though the reds are perhaps the best known. For great examples, look to Campo de Borja DOP, which is situated to the south of the region's Ebro River.

There are four DOP appellations in Aragon; look for wines from Somontano, the most northern. It produces wines in a wide range of styles, with international grape varieties such as Cabernet Sauvignon being authorised to be grown here.

Common varietals in Aragon DOP wines

White	Red
Alcañon	Cabernet Sauvignon
Chardonnay	Garnacha Tinta
Garnacha Blanca	Merlot
Gewürztraminer	Moristel
Macabeo	Parraleta
Riesling	Pinot Noir
Sauvignon Blanc	Syrah
	Tempranillo

Castilla y León

Spain's largest wine-producing region, Castilla y León, is situated in the north-west of the country and contains nine DOP appellations. One of the few Spanish winemaking areas that doesn't have a coast, Castilla y León forms part of the Meseta Central plateau, notable for its long, hot summers and cool evenings, which help to slow down the ripening process of the grapes.

The region is known for producing wonderful reds from the Tempranillo grape, particularly those from the Ribera del Duero DOP, which is situated along the Duero River. Though some 100 per cent Tempranillo wines are produced here, many of the region's best-regarded wines are blended with Cabernet Sauvignon, Merlot and Malbec to produce Bordeaux-style blends that are highly esteemed the world over. Ribera del Duero wines are notable for their ability to develop and improve over time and many high-quality examples will benefit significantly from a little aging.

The region is lesser known for its white wines, but fine examples made with Verdejo grapes can be found. Rueda DOP is perhaps the best-known area for quality white wines, where grapes are grown at high altitudes for a dry finish that is rich in herbal aromas.

Common varietals in Castilla y León DOP wines

White	Red
Verdejo	Tempranillo
Viura	Cabernet Sauvignon
Sauvignon Blanc	Merlot
Palomino	Syrah
Viognier	Garnacha
Chardonnay	

Catalunya

Catalunya (also known as Catalonia) is one of the country's most important wine regions and is known around the world for its signature sparkling wine, Cava, of which Catalunya is responsible for producing over 90 per cent of Spain's output.

Situated along the Mediterranean coast of north-eastern Spain, Catalunya is covered by a single umbrella DOP, meaning that all its wines are granted DOP status. Within the region there are 10 smaller DOP regions, including Priorat, one of only two regions in Spain granted the coveted DOCa (see page 138).

Priorat is notable for its volcanic soil, which enriches the grapes with a rich minerality that carries through to the delicious wines produced here. Annual yields are closely monitored and the amount of wine coming out of Priorat is relatively small, which only adds to its desirability. The wines of the area are generally red and are made with either Garnacha or Carignan grapes. Single-varietal wines are the most common, but blends that use either of these two grapes as a base do occur.

The area's famous sparkling wine, Cava, is largely produced in the DOP of Penedès, situated close to the city of Barcelona. Much like Champagne, Cava is made using the *méthode traditionnelle* (see page 5), which sets it apart from other sparkling wines. It presents a mouth-puckering acidity and lean, clean finish that sparkling wine afficionados love. As an alternative to Champagne, and along with Crémant, Cava ranks among the best and most affordable.

Common varietals in Catalunya DOP wines

White	Red
Chardonnay	Garnacha
Macabeo	Carignan
Xarel-lo	Tempranillo
Parellada	Pinot Noir
Garnacha Blanca	Trepat

Galicia

Known for its crisp, fragrant white wines made from Albariño grapes, Galicia is situated in the north-west of Spain. In a country known for its arid heat, Galicia is notable for its high rainfall, Atlantic breezes and long hours of sun, which combine to give the area its high humidity. This seems to agree with the grapes grown here as the area produces more grapes each year than almost any other winemaking region in Europe.

There are five DOP appellations within Galicia, with the best known being Rias Baixas, which exports a significant amount of its wine to the international market. It is known for producing wonderfully crisp and acidic whites from Albariño grapes. These wines are often characterised by having a slight fizz on the tongue, similar to Portugal's Vinho Verde wines (page 133).

The area's red wines haven't made a mark on the international market and aren't particularly notable in a country where much wonderful red wine is made, but good examples can be found, with Caiño Tinto, Mencía and Tempranillo being the most-planted red varietals.

Common varietals in Galicia DOP wines

White	Red
Albariño	Caiño Tinto
Loureira Blanca	Espadeiro
Treixadura	Loureira Tinta
Caiño Blanco/Branco	Sousón
Godello	Mencía
Doña Blanca	Brancellao
Blanca de Monterrei	Merenzao
	Tempranillo

Madrid

The vineyards situated around Spain's capital city are covered by a single DOP, Vino de Madrid. Madrid's climate is typified by hot, dry summers, with temperatures often climbing as high as 40°C/104°F.

The area is divided between three sub-regions, each at different altitudes. The largest of these is Arganda, which is home to around half of Madrid's vineyards. The second largest is San Martin, which sits in the shadow of the Sierra de Gredos mountain range and receives the highest rainfall of the region as a result. The third region, and the smallest in terms of wine production, is Navalcarnero, which is situated on the flatter land to the south-west of Madrid.

The area is mainly known for its red wines, with the highest regarded being from made from Garnacha grapes. White wine, typically made from lightly aromatic Albillo grapes, is also produced, though in smaller amounts. Bottles of Madrid white wines are harder to come by outside of the region itself.

Common varietals in Madrid DOP wines

White
Albillo
Malvar

Red
Garnacha Tinto
Tempranillo

Murcia

One of Spain's smaller wine regions, both in terms of geography and notoriety, Murcia is situated in the south-east of Spain on the Mediterranean coast. Home to three DOP appellations, it is best known for its full-bodied reds made from the Monastrell grape.

The coastal areas of the region are cooled by breezes from the Mediterranean, but this soon gives way to the unforgiving heat of Spain's central region. This heat makes the area unsuitable for growing much in the way of white grapes, though Macabeo and Airén grapes are grown here, the latter of which are mainly vinified for making brandy.

When looking to Murcia, your best bet is to stick with the region's signature reds, particularly those from the DOP regions of Bullas, Yecla and Jumilla. The Monastrell grape thrives in these warm, dry climates and is used to produce a fine fruit-forward wine that is high in tannins and can benefit from a little aging. Monastrell can be found as a single-varietal wine, though is often blended with Tempranillo to soften its edges.

Common varietals in Murcia DOP wines

White
Macabeo

Red
Monastrell
Tempranillo

Navarra

This landlocked region in central northern Spain is primarily known for its signature rosé (*rosado*) wines, which are often, though not exclusively, made with Garnacha grapes. These wines are typically fragrant with ripe fruit flavours and offer a very different rosé experience to, say, the lean, mineralistic Provencal rosés that have become so popular in recent years. The area contains a single DOP (Navarra DOP), covering the southern half of the region, with a very small part of this region also crossing over with Rioja DOCa (see pages 149–50).

Though Navarra's pink wines have long been its most famous product, its Tempranillo-based red wines have garnered more attention in recent years. However, these are still often overshadowed by the wines of its much more famous neighbour, Rioja.

The production of white wine in the area is limited, though examples of Chardonnay, Macabeo and Garnacha Blanca can be found locally.

Common varietals in Navarra DOP wines

White
Chardonnay
Macabeo

Red
Garnacha
Tempranillo
Cabernet Sauvignon
Merlot
Pinot Noir

Rioja

The most famous of all Spanish wine regions, Rioja is also one of only two regions to have been granted the coveted DOCa classification, which signifies wines of real quality, produced over a sustained period of time.

The area is split into three sub-regions, with wines often made from a blended variety of grapes to achieve the perfect balance. Grapes grown in Rioja Alta tend to be more fruit-forward, those from Rioja Alavesa are richer and have greater acidity and those from Rioja Oriental are dark in colour with a higher alcohol content.

Rioja is made in both red and white styles. While both are highly regarded, it is the full-bodied red that is most synonymous with the region. Because of the region's DOCa status, wine production here is highly scrutinised to protect the quality and reputation of the wines. Traditionally there were four red and three white grape varietals approved for the production of Rioja (see below), but a handful of other varietals have since been approved for inclusion, although strict maximum limits were set as to how much of a wine could be made up of these new varietals.

Rioja Classifications

To further protect the quality of Rioja DOCa wines, the region uses its own classification system to rank the wines that it produces, with wines in the higher tiers fetching a higher price. These classifications will be clearly labelled on any bottle of Rioja. From highest to lowest, the tiers are:

Generico

These are young Rioja wines that are generally sold within the first two years after the grapes have been harvested. These wines tend to be fruit-forward with mouth-puckering acidity.

Crianza

These wines have spent at least one year aging in oak barrels before being bottled. They tend to be richer and more tannic than Generico wines, with the flavours of rich red fruit and an undercurrent of leather.

Reserva

Wines labelled as Reserva are made with grapes grown during a notably superior growing season, and with only the finest grapes of that season. These wines are aged for at least three years, with a minimum of one year being spent in oak barrels. These wines are softer and more supple than younger Riojas, with notes of dried fruit and tobacco coming through.

Gran Reserva

Similar to Reserva wines, but made with grapes harvested in only the very finest vintage years. These wines are aged in oak for a minimum of two years and then in the bottle for a minimum of three years, making the youngest Gran Reserva wines five years old at the time of sale. Gran Reserva wines account for just a fraction of Rioja sold and can fetch high prices as a result.

Common varietals in Rioja DOCa wines

White

Macabeo
Malvasia
Garnacha Blanca
Maturana Blanca
Tempranillo Blanco
Torrontés
Chardonnay
Sauvignon Blanc
Verdejo

Red

Tempranillo
Garnacha Tinta
Mazuelo
Graciano
Maturana Tinta

Valencia

Situated on the hot eastern coast of Spain, Valencia contains just one DOC appellation that covers the whole region. The warm climate and low rainfall do not immediately lend themselves to the slow-ripening of grapes needed to produce good-quality wines, but there is quality to be found here. Look for wines from the area of Alto Turia, where the cooler temperatures of its higher location are beneficial for growing the white grapes Macabeo and Merseguera.

Perhaps the region's best-known wine export is the sweet and aromatic Moscatel de Valencia, a dessert wine that is rich with the flavour of honeyed melon and uses Valencia's long hours of sun to its advantage.

The region is also home to some easy-drinking, if not remarkable, red wines, made from Monastrell, Garnacha, Tempranillo and Merlot grapes. The warm climate produces bold, fruit-forward red wines that are full-bodied and relatively high in alcohol.

Common varietals in Valencia DOP wines

White
Macabeo
Merseguera
Moscatel

Red
Monastrell
Garnacha
Tempranillo
Merlot

The United Kingdom

Until recently, wine from the UK was seen as something of a novelty. The British climate was too cool and wet to produce consistent high-quality yields, and winemaking was more of a hobby than a serious industry. In the last 10 years, however, this has all changed, with the British wine industry being one of the few beneficiaries of the climate change crisis.

The UK's climate has been getting steadily warmer, with some areas of southern England achieving the kind of steady summer temperatures that have been traditionally associated with some of France's best-known wine-producing areas, especially those that specialise in growing cooler-climate grapes, such as Champagne.

Though this is worrying on a global scale, it does create a new outlook for the UK's wine industry – which, though small, is one of the world's fastest growing and is becoming increasingly associated with high-quality wines. Sparkling wine in particular, which accounts for almost 70 per cent of all wine produced in the UK, is fast gaining a reputation for being world-class. Producers of English sparkling wine have focused largely on the same grapes used in the production of Champagne – Chardonnay, Pinot Noir and Pinot Meunier – and many use the same labour-intensive traditional method as Champagne in their production (see page 5). Because of this, English sparkling wines from well-regarded producers, such as Nyetimber, Rathfinny, Chapel Down, Hambledon and Gusbourne, among others, can fetch

Wales

East Anglia

Kent

Surrey

Sussex
South Downs

Hampshire
South Downs

prices that rival their French counterparts, and are becoming increasingly sought out by wine drinkers around the world.

Much of UK wine production is grouped around the south-eastern counties of England, with Kent, Sussex, Hampshire and Surrey being hotspots for English sparkling wine. Over 60 per cent of the UK's wine comes from the south-east, with central southern England, the south-west and East Anglia making up the bulk of the remaining production.

Sussex is particularly well suited to the growing of vines as, being situated in the far south-east of England, it receives lower rainfall than other areas. The area's soil is rich with limestone, which promotes a good amount of acidity in the grapes that are grown there. The soil and climate of the region, especially around the South Downs, carries many parallels with France's Champagne region. It is perhaps no wonder then that Sussex's wineries were the UK's first to be granted PDO status, in June 2022 (see below).

Outside of England, Wales is the only other country within the UK to have really made a mark on the nation's wine scene, though the level of production is minimal when compared to England. As the UK climate continues to change and temperatures rise throughout the British Isles, however, other areas of the UK will start to become viable for growing grapes.

As yet, British wine is dominated by sparkling and still white wines, with the climate not suited to the long ripening of red wine grapes. The exception to this is Pinot Noir, which thrives in cooler climates, and it is possible to find good-quality reds, though the vast majority of the Pinot Noir grapes grown in the UK are used for sparkling wine.

UK Wine Classifications

Like much of the rest of Europe, the UK operates a three-tier system for classifying its wines. Running from top to bottom, these are:

PDO (Protected Designation of Origin)

This is the top tier of wines produced within the UK and the most closely monitored in terms of production. PDO wines must be made with 100 per cent grapes that are grown within the country marked on the bottle's label (either England or Wales). Grapes must be from a list of permitted UK varietals (of which there are around 90 for still wines and only 6 for sparkling wines). No hybrid vine varieties are permitted to be used. Wines that apply for this designation must undergo independent testing to check for quality before they are granted PDO status. These wines are labelled as either 'English Quality Wine' or 'Welsh Quality Wine' depending on where they are produced.

PGI (Protected Geographical Indication)

Wines that are classed using this middle tier of British wine must be labelled as 'English Regional Wine' or 'Welsh Regional Wine', depending on where they are produced. Eighty-five per cent of the grapes used must be from the demarked country, while the remaining 15 per cent can come from anywhere in the UK. Again, there are around 90 permitted grape varietals for both still and sparkling wine but, unlike for PDO wines, hybrid varietals are permitted. Wines that apply for this designation must undergo independent testing to check for quality before they can be granted PGI status.

Varietal Wine

These wines will feature no indication of country of origin on the label, and the grapes can be grown anywhere in the UK. They will feature the grape varietal on the label, and at least 85 per cent of the grapes used in producing the wine must be from that varietal. These wines are not permitted to use the 'English' or 'Welsh' demarcation on their labels. No testing is required to be granted this status.

Common varietals in UK wines

White
Chardonnay
Bacchus
Ortega
Seyval Blanc
Reichensteiner

Red
Pinot Noir
Pinot Meunier

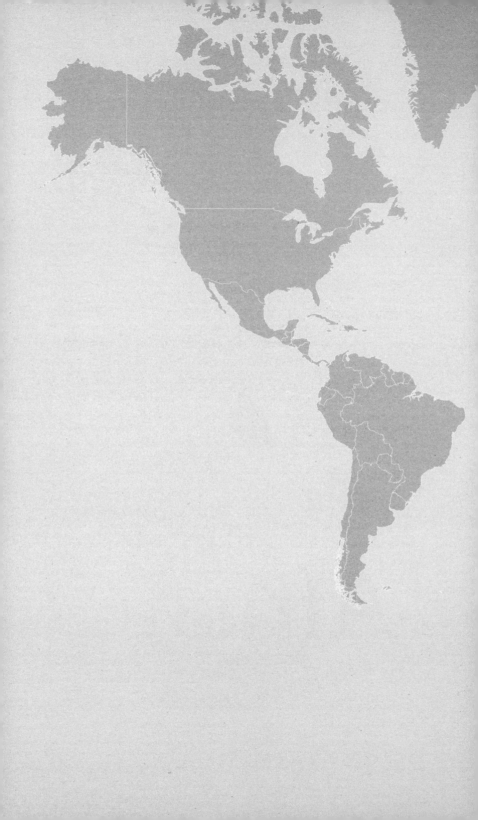

Africa

South Africa

Located at the southern tip of Africa, South Africa is known especially for Pinotage and Chenin Blanc. Though these are undoubtedly the country's signature grapes, there are plenty of other fine wines to explore, including Cabernet Sauvignon, Colombard, Shiraz, Sauvignon Blanc and Chardonnay.

The most highly regarded and prolific wine regions are found in the country's Western Cape, where grapes are cooled by the refreshing breezes coming in from the Indian and Atlantic Oceans. The Western Cape is one of six Geographical Units (see page 162) demarked for the production of South African wine, but its climate and topography are so ideal that it is responsible for producing over 90 per cent of South Africa's wines.

South African Pinotage, a hybrid grape bred in the country from Pinot Noir and Cinsault, has the potential to be beautifully rich and full of spice and red fruit when treated well, though poor-quality versions have been likened to paint stripper and as a result the wine has fallen somewhat out of fashion. In recent years, however, the quality and popularity of the wine is on the rise, with examples from the Stellenbosch region (located in the Western Cape) being among the most highly regarded.

Chenin Blanc is the country's widest-planted grape varietal. Originally from the Loire Valley in France, this grape thrives in South Africa's varied landscape, where in Afrikaans it was known as Steen. Chenin Blanc can present in many styles, from fresh and fruity to intensely dry and even late-harvest sweet varieties. Knowing which style is in your bottle is a slightly inexact science, though many South African wine producers provide a helpful amount of information on the label.

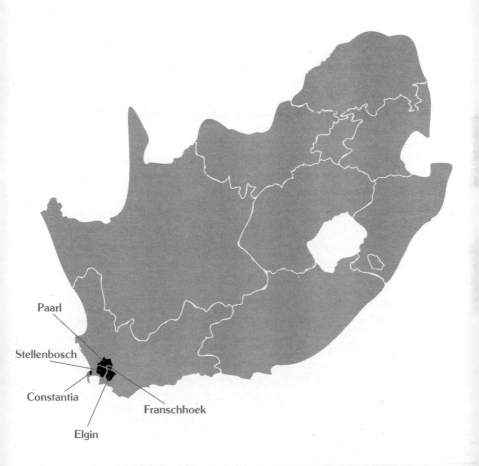

Paarl

Stellenbosch

Constantia

Franschhoek

Elgin

South African Wine Classifications

South Africa's WO (Wine of Origin) scheme is a layered appellation system, with different levels of geographical indication nested within each other.

Similarly to the USA, Australia and New Zealand, South Africa does not restrict the grape varietals that can be grown in each area, and growers are free to plant what they choose. Wines labelled with a GU, region, district or ward must contain 100 per cent grapes grown within that geographical indication. Wines labelled with a vintage or varietal must contain 85 per cent grapes grown within that year or from that specified varietal.

Working from the outside inward, the production areas for wines are categorised as the following:

GUs (Geographical Units)
Almost all wine made in South Africa is produced in one of six GUs. These are large overarching regions that may contain many variations in terms of *terroir* within them but equally have some defining characteristics in terms of landscape, climate and soil type. The current regions are the Western Cape, the Northern Cape, the Eastern Cape, KwaZulu-Natal, Limpopo and the Free State. Of these, the Western Cape is by far the most important in terms of wine production.

Regions

The next level down is regions, with the most important GUs being carved into several sub-regions. For example, the Western Cape GU is subdivided into six regions, each with a homogenous climate or landscape to help wine buyers further mine down into where the wine in their bottle came from. A good example here is the Coastal Region, which is located within the Western Cape GU and covers all wines produced with that maritime climate.

Districts

As a general rule, wine regions can then be divided again into districts, which are smaller areas again and, as such, contain more unifying characteristics.

Wards

Going smaller again, districts are subdivided into wards, which are the smallest geographical areas that the WO scheme recognises. That said, some wines will be labelled with a specific estate or vineyard, in which case, 100 per cent of the grapes in those bottles will be from those specific locations.

It is worth noting that this Russian-doll nesting system doesn't always work as neatly as we might like and there are exceptions to these rules, the occasional wards that do not sit inside districts, such as Prince Albert Valley, being one notable example.

South African wine regions

Constantia
(Western Cape, Coastal Region)
Famous for producing a sweet dessert wine from Muscat grapes, but also home to some excellent Rieslings.

Elgin
(Western Cape, Cape South Coast, Overberg)
Situated 40 miles to the south-east of Cape Town, Elgin has a cool climate fuelled by breezes from the South Atlantic, making it ideal for grapes that enjoy a long growing season. The wines are often aromatic and expressive of their *terroir*. Fine examples of Sauvignon Blanc and Chardonnay can be found here.

Franschhoek
(Western Cape)
This valley is well known for its beefy Shiraz and Cabernet Sauvignons. Sheltered from maritime breezes by two mountain ranges, the wines here are distinct from those produced in the Coastal Region and enjoy a long growing season that brings out a complex flavour in the grapes. It also produces aromatic, fruity white wines and Pinot Noir/Chardonnay sparkling blends.

Paarl
(Western Cape, Coastal Region)
This district contains three wards, located around 40 miles inland from Cape Town. The vines grow on low mountain slopes in rocky granite soil that is well-suited to rich and robust red wine grapes such as Cabernet Sauvignon, Syrah (Shiraz) and Pinotage.

Stellenbosch
(Western Cape, Coastal Region)
This prolific area is located just east of Cape Town and contains seven wards. It produces excellent-quality Pinotage, as well as big blended reds in the style of Bordeaux.

Varietals common to South Africa

White
Chenin Blanc
Chardonnay
Sauvignon Blanc
Colombard
Riesling
Muscat

Red
Pinotage
Cabernet Sauvignon
Shiraz (Syrah)
Merlot

The
Americas

Argentina

Known for its big beefy reds, Argentinian wine first became a major player on the international wine scene in the late 1990s when the country's signature Malbecs started gaining in popularity.

Though Argentina has a long coastline, the majority of its grapes are grown inland. The Andes Mountains create a rain shadow that protects the grapes from high rainfall, and the vineyards here are positioned at some of the highest altitudes in the world. These high altitudes mean that the grapes get long hours of exposure to the sun, ripen slower than they would in lower, warmer locations and develop thick skins, which give Argentinian Malbecs their distinctive chewy tannins and rich fruit flavours.

For Argentine white wines, look to Torrontés, the country's signature white grape. The region of La Rioja (not to be confused with the Spanish region of Rioja, pages 149–50), where the grapes are again grown at high altitudes, produces full-flavoured versions with lip-smacking acidity.

La Rioja

Cuyo

Mendoza

Patagonia

Argentine Wine Classifications

As in many New World wine countries, wine produced in Argentina is fairly loosely regulated in terms of the grape varietals grown within a specific area and the production methods used to make the wine. The exception to this is some Malbecs, which are more closely monitored, perhaps because of the grape's worldwide popularity and importance to the export market.

There are currently two recognised Denominación de Origen Controlada (DOCs) for Malbec, both situated within the sub-region Mendoza in central west Argentina. Malbecs labelled as either Luján de Cuyo DOC or San Rafael DOC are closely regulated. Not all Argentine Malbecs are covered by these DOCs, however, so it is worth checking the label for this extra marker of quality.

Outside of these DOC classifications, Argentine wines will generally fall into one of two categories:

Indicación Geográfica (Geographic Indication/IG)
A wine with this designation must be produced within one of around 100 recognised wine appellations in Argentina. Wines marked with a specific IG must be made of at least 80 per cent of the grape varietal that the wine is labelled as (e.g. Malbec), and 85 per cent of the grapes used must have been grown within that IG. Outside of the DOC wines, this classification is the easiest way to identify a quality Argentine wine. When exploring Argentina's IG appellations, Paraje Altamira GI and San Pablo GI are a good place to start, with both producing high-quality Malbec from grapes that thrive in the high altitudes that both areas enjoy.

Indicación de Procedencia (Indication of Origin/IP)

This lower tier of wine classification is given to wines that are labelled solely with one of Argentina's three larger wine-producing areas (all of which the much smaller appellations marked on IG wines sit within). These are the Northern Regions, Cuyo and Patagonia. If your wine is labelled with one of these as its only geographical indicator, it is likely to be of a lower quality than an IG wine.

Varietals common to Argentina

White
Pedro Giménez
Torrontés
Moscatel

Red
Malbec
Bonarda
Cabernet Sauvignon

Chile

The fifth-biggest wine producer in the world, Chile
is known for producing accessible, budget-friendly
bottles on a grand scale. That doesn't mean that
there isn't great quality to be found here, too, and
in recent years the wines of Chile have been gaining
greater respect from wine drinkers around the world.

The landscape of Chile is dominated by two major
factors: its dramatic Pacific coastline that runs the length
of the country to the west and the Andes Mountains that
form the backbone of the country to the east.

The country produces a wide range of popular wine
styles and, as such, it can be hard to identify those that
are elevated from the easy-drinking, everyday wines
that make up the majority of Chile's output. The wines
here are very affordable, though, so mistakes are rarely
expensive and, in fact, spending a bit more money on a
Chilean wine typically ensures that you're purchasing
something of higher quality. For red wines, the country
produces some excellent Cabernet Sauvignon, with wines
from the Central Valley, particularly the sub-region of
Rapel Valley, being of notably high quality.

Atacama

Coquimbo

Aconcagua

Central Valley

Southern
Chile

Another red grape that is worth seeking out is Carménère, an aromatic and spicy red that can be difficult to handle but that does well in the Chilean climate. Look for wines from the Colchagua Valley, also a sub-region of the Central Valley, for good examples.

Though Chile is best known for its red wines, more than a third of wine produced in the country is white, with good examples of Sauvignon Blanc, Chardonnay, Muscat and Riesling all available. Chilean Sauvignon Blanc is floral and fruit-forward, closer to New Zealand Sauvignon Blancs in style than the grassy, mineral varieties of the Loire Valley.

Chilean Wine Classifications

The country is split into five official wine-producing regions, which are, running north to south, Atacama, Coquimbo, Aconcagua, the Central Valley and Southern Chile. Each of these larger regions is sub-divided into smaller appellations and, like the labelling systems of the USA and Argentina, the more specific a wine label is about the origin of a wine, the more likely it is that the wine is of a high quality.

Denominaciónes de Origen (Denominations of Origin/DOs)

Chile's wine regions (DOs), which were only established as recently as 1995, are used to ensure that some rules are followed as to what's in the bottle. Similar to the US system, there are no restrictions as to which grapes can be grown in each area, though wines that are labelled with a DO must be made of 75 per cent grapes from within that region and those labelled with a varietal must contain at least 75 per cent of that grape. For wines that are exported, which accounts for well over half of the wine produced in the country, this percentage goes up to 85 per cent. In terms of where to start, the Maipo Valley and Colchagua DOs are notable for Carménère and red wine blends. For white wines, look to areas close to the coast, such as Casablanca Valley DO which is known for its Chardonnay and Sauvignon Blanc.

Varietals common to Chile

White	Red
Chardonnay	Pais
Sauvignon Blanc	Cabernet Sauvignon
Sauvignon Vert	Merlot
Sémillon	Carménère
Riesling	Zinfandel
Muscat	Pinot Noir
Syrah	

USA

The USA is now recognised as home to some of the world's finest producers, and it is the fourth-largest producer of wine after Italy, France and Spain. Wine arrived in the USA with European settlers in the sixteenth century, first made from grapes that were native to the country, but soon after from imported grapevines, planted for the purpose of making wine.

The Americans are also a nation of wine drinkers, with the country being the world's largest consumer of wine, both home-grown US vintages and wines imported from elsewhere, with over a quarter of wine consumed in the country being imported.

Washington State

Oregon

California

Without question, the United States' most important and prolific wine-producing region is California, which produces over 80 per cent of the country's wine. A statistic that is even more impressive when set against the fact that each of the USA's 50 states produces some sort of wine, including those with climates that would not immediately recommend themselves to wine production, such as Alaska.

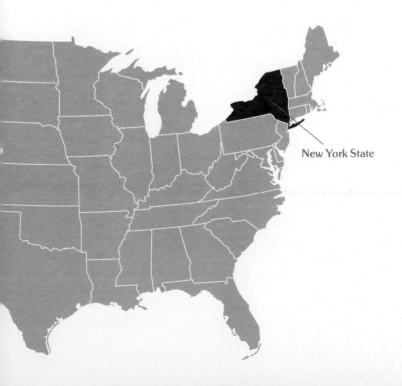

New York State

US Wine Classifications

The US appellation system is based around designated AVAs (American Viticultural Areas). The rules that govern what grapes are grown and how wine is made are far less strict than those in European countries. Because of this, US wine has a reputation for exciting, experimental producers who are able to play with grape varietals and production methods in a way that simply wouldn't be allowed in many European countries.

Wines generally have the grape varietal clearly identified on the label, so a lot of the informed guesswork that is involved in purchasing European wines isn't a factor when it comes to wines from the USA. But here are a few tips:

Wines that are labelled by AVA will contain at least 85 per cent of grapes grown within that region. If wines are labelled by a wider state or simply as 'product of the USA', this minimum percentage goes down to 75 per cent.

Wines that identify a specific vineyard are made of at least 95 per cent grapes grown within that vineyard, so with US wines, the more specific an area is given, the more confident you can be on the provenance of the grapes. Likewise, if a wine is labelled as containing a single grape varietal, it must be made from at least 75 per cent grapes of that varietal. AVA wines labelled with a specific vintage must be made from 95 per cent grapes from within that AVA harvested in that particular year.

This may sound complicated, but really all it means is that the more information a label gives you in terms of location, vintage and grape varietal, the more likely it is to be a good-quality wine.

The Judgment of Paris, 1976

A turning point for American wines, and one that first gave them recognition and acceptance on the world stage, was the Judgment of Paris in 1976. This was a blind wine-tasting competition organised to celebrate 200 years of the US republic, and which pitted Californian wines against their French counterparts. Californian Cabernet Sauvignons and Chardonnays went head-to-head with some of France's most revered Bordeaux and white Burgundy wines, and surprised the world by coming out on top. The film *Bottle Shock* with Alan Rickman is a great watch and tells the extraordinary story.

US wine regions

California

California is the hub of the American wine industry, with a diverse geography that incorporates many different microclimates and landscapes. This makes the state suited to growing many different grape varietals and producing wine in a variety of styles; in fact, the state is responsible for more than 80 per cent of the country's wine output. There are over 450 different grape varietals grown in California and the area is divided into 139 AVAs (which is over half of all AVAs currently in the USA).

The consistently warm weather produces very ripe grapes that, in turn, are used to produce fruit-forward wines with a slightly higher than average alcohol content. California is best known for its red wines, with bold Cabernet Sauvignons, Merlots, Zinfandels and Pinot Noirs taking centre stage.

White wine in the area is dominated by Chardonnay, with classic examples being heavily oaked, buttery rich and redolent of vanilla and subtle spice. These wines, though once popular, have become increasingly out of fashion on the international wine scene, with the clean minerality of French Chardonnays, particularly those produced in Burgundy, being more suited to our current tastes. If you look beyond mass-produced wines that dominate supermarket shelves, though, you will find some wonderful examples of Californian Chardonnay that are far subtler on the palate and are made with great skill and finesse.

The best-known wine-producing areas are situated close to the Pacific Ocean, where the warm weather is tempered by cool breezes. The Napa Valley AVA is perhaps the most famous of all the Californian sub-regions and is responsible for producing much of California's world-class wine. Its unique *terroir*, with soil rich in volcanic minerals, makes it specially suited to growing grapes that impart a complexity of structure and flavour to the wines produced here.

Varietals common to California

White
Chardonnay
Sauvignon Blanc

Red
Merlot
Cabernet Sauvignon
Pinot Noir
Syrah (Shiraz)
Zinfandel

New York State

When most people picture New York, vineyards are far from the first thing that springs to mind, but the region is actually the USA's third-biggest producer, with the Finger Lakes and Long Island forming the backbone of New York State's wine industry.

New York is based on the East Coast and, as such, has a much colder climate and harsher winters than the other wine regions covered in these pages. Because of this, the European grape varietals that have thrived elsewhere in the USA do not do as well here and up to 90 per cent of grapes grown in New York State are from varietals native to the USA. These native grapes are generally regarded as being of inferior quality and, as such, are used in the production of Communion wine and non-alcoholic grape juice.

This isn't to say that New York wines aren't worth seeking out. The small percentage of European-style grapes that are grown here, such as Riesling, have produced some superior-quality wines that are starting to put New York wines on the map.

Varietals common to New York

White	Red
Riesling	Cabernet Franc
Sauvignon Blanc	Merlot
Niagara	Concord
Catawba	

Oregon

The smallest of the USA's wine-producing areas that we are
going to explore, Oregon is responsible for around 1 per
cent of wine produced in the country. Though small in terms
of output, Oregon has garnered a strong reputation on the
international wine stage, where it has been recognised for its
quality production methods and the reflected standards of
its wine.

Oregon is made up of 18 AVAs, with six of these located in the
Willamette Valley, which is surrounded by mountain ranges to
the north, east and west. This makes the area suited for grape
growing as the valley is protected from the state's otherwise
relatively high rainfall. Wineries within the Willamette Valley
produce mostly Pinot Noirs, which have garnered international
acclaim for their distinctive rich, spicy flavour and are relatively
affordable for wines of such high quality.

Varietals common to Oregon

White
Pinot Gris

Red
Pinot Noir

Washington State

Washington is the second-largest producer of wine in the USA, though it is only responsible for 5 per cent of all wine produced. Compared to California, the area isn't particularly well known on the international export market, though its wines are worth seeking out as it makes many different styles very well. Of particular note are Washington's red wines, particularly those made with Syrah or Sangiovese grapes, which are full of the flavours of ripe autumnal fruits and have a tannic backbone that is well suited to aging.

The vast majority of the grapes grown in Washington are planted in the eastern part of the state, in the shadow of the Cascade mountain range, which protects grapes from the wetter maritime climate coming in from the west. There are around 20 AVAs in Washington State.

Around two-thirds of the wine produced in Washington is red, while the bulk of the remainder is white, with a little given over to rosé production. There are over 80 different grape varietals grown in the area, with the most common being Cabernet Sauvignon, Merlot and Syrah for the reds and Chardonnay, Riesling and Pinot Gris for the whites.

Varietals common to Washington

White	Red
Chardonnay	Cabernet Sauvignon
Riesling	Merlot
Sauvignon Blanc	Syrah (Shiraz)
Gewürztraminer	Sangiovese

Australia

Australia

Though a relatively young winemaking nation – wine grapes first arrived in Australia in the eighteenth century – wine is a key part of Australian culture and the country is one of the world's largest exporters of wine.

It is known for the mass-market wines that dominate the supermarket shelves, but there are many fine examples to be found too, the most famous being the superlative Penfolds Grange, which remains one of the world's most coveted and collectable wines.

Australian wine regions are divided into set Geographical Indications (GIs), similar to France's appellation system, though they are far less rigid in terms of the rules around winemaking practices. There are around 65 GIs in Australia, and wine bearing the name of any of these must contain at least 85 per cent grapes grown within that specific area. There are no rules over which grapes can be grown within each GI; however, because the country is so large, with such a varied climate and landscape, different regions specialise in different varietals.

Though much of the country is very dry, winemakers have harnessed the country's rivers to provide irrigation for their vines, which is why many of the country's renowned winemaking areas are sited close to rivers.

Western Australia

South Australia

New South Wales

Victoria

Tasmania

Australian wine regions

New South Wales

New South Wales is the second-biggest wine-producing region in Australia, with much of its production given over to mass-produced wines that dominate supermarket shelves around the world. This isn't to say that there aren't wonderful wines to be found here, with examples of world-class Sémillon and age-worthy Shiraz produced in abundance.

The area's best-known region is undoubtedly the Hunter Valley, which is often seen as a jumping-off point for tourists looking to explore Australia's wineries due to its proximity to Sydney. The region's notable Sémillon wines present lower alcohol levels of around 10% ABV due to the technique of picking the grapes while slightly underripe. These wines are often oaked for long periods before bottling and are rich with vanilla and spice in the glass.

The workhorse of the region is the Big Rivers GI, which is responsible for delivering many of the mass-produced and box wines that Australia is known for around the world. The vines here are high-yielding and predominantly given over to growing the ever popular Chardonnay and Shiraz.

Varietals common to New South Wales

White	Red
Chardonnay	Pinot Noir
Sauvignon Blanc	Shiraz
Sémillon	Cabernet Sauvignon
Pinot Gris	Merlot

South Australia

Responsible for producing over half of the wine made in in the country, South Australia is the heartland of Australian winemaking. The climate varies from dry and warm in the summer months to mild and wet in the winter months, giving the area a climate reminiscent of the Mediterranean. The area is home to some of Australia's best-known wine regions and producers, especially the Barossa Valley and its spicy Shiraz wines. White wines in the area tend to be high in sugar and low in acid, though some world-class examples of Chardonnay, Sémillon and Riesling can be found.

The Barossa Valley is home to one of the oldest living vineyards in the world, the Old Garden, with the Mourvedre vines planted in 1853. The vines here have survived for so long because the grape phylloxera, a microscopic insect that feasts on the roots of grapevines and is the bane of wine producers worldwide, is currently not present in the region. The Barossa Valley and its neighbour Eden Valley are a unique landscape: the lowest points of these valleys are warm, resulting in rich, fruity wines with big tannins, whereas the higher slopes are cooler and result in wines with higher acidity and subtler notes of fruit.

Varietals common to South Australia

With no restrictions on what grapes can be grown region to region, there are over 50 different varietals grown in South Australia. Those listed below are the most common.

White	Red
Riesling	Shiraz (Syrah)
Chardonnay	Cabernet Sauvignon
Sémillon	Grenache
Sauvignon Blanc	Merlot
Viognier	Mourvedre

Grape phylloxera: the pest that nearly killed the wine trade

Phylloxera are tiny transparent insects, similar in appearance to aphids, that feed on sap from the roots and leaves of grapevines. Once a vine is infested, there is no cure and the insects will spread from vine to vine with devastating results.

Towards the end of the nineteenth century, when phylloxera were accidentally introduced to Europe from the Americas, a great plague of the insects swept across the continent, killing up to two-thirds of all European vines. France was the worst affected nation, with the plague bringing the wine industry to its knees and many winemakers never recovering from the loss.

It was eventually discovered that in America, where grape phylloxera had originated, many vines had developed the ability to at least partially protect themselves from the pest. To battle the threat of phylloxera, European vines were grafted to the rootstock from resistant American vines as a means of protection – a solution that is still used to this day and one that doubtlessly saved the European wine industry. It is because of phylloxera that the world's oldest vines are now found in regions where the insects have not taken hold, such as western and southern Australia.

Tasmania

Set apart from the Australian mainland, the island of Tasmania sits to the south of the country's other winemaking regions and, as a result, produces wines with a character that is distinct from those of its northern counterparts. The climate here is cooler than mainland Australia's, with strong sea winds coming in from all sides of the island. Because of this, many of the grapes cultivated here have to be grown behind protective screens to prevent them from becoming damaged. It also means that the grapes here spend longer on the vine and can be more expressive of the *terroir* of the region as a result.

Though the region has a relatively small output, in recent years Tasmanian wines have become increasingly recognised for their quality at an international level. Climate change has definitely played a part in this, with the poor weather that was once a threat to producers becoming a rarer occurrence, meaning that yields and quality have become more consistent.

Tasmania's lower temperatures make it well suited for the production of sparkling wines, most commonly made from a blend of Chardonnay and Pinot Noir grapes using the *méthode traditionnelle*. The island is also home to great-quality examples of other cool-climate wines, including Pinot Noir, Sauvignon Blanc, Riesling and Chardonnay.

Varietals common to Tasmania

White
Chardonnay
Sauvignon Blanc
Pinot Gris
Riesling
Gewürztraminer

Red
Pinot Noir
Cabernet Sauvignon
Merlot

Victoria

Situated in south-east Australia, below New South Wales, Victoria has more wineries than any other Australian region yet ranks third in terms of overall production.

Perhaps the most refined wines come from the region's southern half, around its capital city, Melbourne. The Yarra Valley in particular is well known for producing top-notch Chardonnay and Pinot Noir. The Chardonnay here is of special note as the cooler climate allows for the production of leaner, cleaner varieties than those produced in most of the rest of Australia, which are often fruit-forward and heavily oaked.

To the south-west of Melbourne, Geelong is known for producing high-quality Pinot Noir and Shiraz (Syrah), as well as Chardonnay. The cool winds coming off the Bass Strait mean that grapes here have a longer growing season and are very expressive of their *terroir* as a result.

Just south of Melbourne, the Mornington Peninsula is another of the state's most notable wine regions. The area is known for its long, dry summers, extensive sunshine and cooling maritime breezes, all of which mean that the growing season here is much longer than in inland areas. The wines here are intense and full of flavour due to their extended time on the vine. The peninsula is known for its Chardonnay and Pinot Noir, but also produces excellent Riesling, Viognier, Cabernet Sauvignon and Shiraz.

Varietals common to Victoria

White	Red
Chardonnay	Pinot Noir
Sauvignon Blanc	Shiraz
Riesling	Cabernet Sauvignon
Pinot Gris	Merlot

Western Australia

Though Western Australia covers a huge area, only the coastal regions to its south-west are known for their wine production. The area enjoys warm summers and mild winters, making it one of Australia's most temperate regions with a climate that closely resembles Bordeaux. Perhaps because if this, a large proportion of the country's fine wines come from here.

Key regions in Western Australia include the Swan Valley and Margaret River, known as one of Australia's finest wine-producing areas and for producing exemplary Cabernet Sauvignons and Chardonnays. The region is also known for its white blends of Sauvignon Blanc and grassy Sémillon (SSB).

Varietals common to Western Australia

White
Chardonnay
Sauvignon Blanc
Sémillon
Riesling

Red
Cabernet Sauvignon
Merlot
Syrah (Shiraz)

New Zealand

Despite its small size, New Zealand punches well above its weight in terms of its importance on the global wine stage. As a winemaking nation it is relatively young, with the industry only really establishing itself in the 1970s, but it is now known around the world for producing world-class Sauvignon Blanc.

As with Australia, New Zealand follows the 85 per cent rule, meaning that for a wine to be labelled with a grape varietal, vintage or region, the wine must be made from at least 85 per cent grapes of that varietal, from that region or grown in that year. Outside of this rule, wine production is largely unregulated, so it can be harder to identify great-quality wines from the label alone.

Almost 80 per cent of all grapes grown in New Zealand are white, and most of these are Sauvignon Blanc, which gives a good idea as to how important the varietal is to the country's wine economy. These wines are crisp and aromatic but tend to be sweeter, with more notes of tropical fruit than their European cousins. The South Island is Sauvignon Blanc country, with the region of Marlborough being the centre of its production and responsible for 90 per cent of the country's output.

The North Island is the warmer of New Zealand's islands, and the majority of the red wines that the country produces come from here. When it comes to reds, New Zealand is notable for producing some soft, silky Pinot Noirs and wonderful varieties of spicy Shiraz (Syrah).

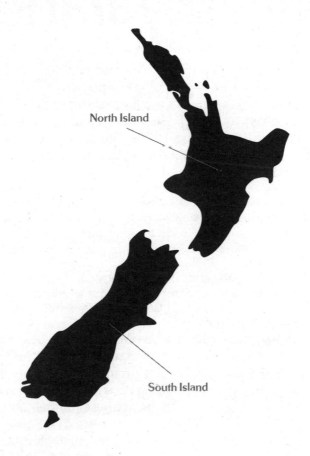

North Island

South Island

Varietals common to New Zealand

White
Sauvignon Blanc
Chardonnay
Riesling

Red
Pinot Noir
Shiraz (Syrah)

Conclusion

It is through our senses that we experience the world, and taking a sip of wine is to truly awaken them. The colour and transparency of the liquid as you hold it up to the light, its weight and texture as you swirl it around our glass, perhaps the sound of bubbles popping as the wine froths and fizzes in its flute, the aroma as you inhale deeply and allow its subtle nuances to awaken your palate and, finally, the exquisite pay-off of taste as you flood your mouth with delicious flavour, bringing all of your other senses into focus. In this way, a glass of wine is a gateway to pleasure and enjoyment. Taste, touch, sound, smell and sight can all trigger memory and, because of your unique bank of memories and experiences, what you experience when you smell and taste that wine might be completely different to the person sitting next you. You might both detect lemon or grassy notes, but perhaps you can also pick up something different, the perfume or aftershave of a long-lost love or the scent of tobacco on your grandfather's clothes as he leant in for a hug. When it comes to wine, so many people go straight for the taste, but 50 per cent of the pleasure is in the nose. Inhale your wine before you taste it and you will unlock aromas and flavours you won't believe.

Once you get a feel for how climate and landscape leave a mark on what's in your glass, it really is possible to travel the world through a glass of wine. Is that Chardonnay lean and mineralistic? Perhaps it's from Burgundy. Is it rich with tropical fruit and notes of vanilla? It might hail from California. It's not an exact science, but it is a fun one, so don't be afraid to make mistakes. It's not a test!

A bottle of wine contains so much more than alcohol; it is the distillation of everything from the grapes on the vine and the hand that held the secateurs that pruned them, to the minerals in the soil and the warmth of the sun. It is a landscape in microcosm, held at a particular moment, waiting for the cork to be unstopped and all of that unique *terroir* to be poured into a glass and savoured. You don't have to understand how wine is made or where it comes from to enjoy it, but I do hope that the information in this book will give you the thirst to find out a bit more and continue your own love affair with wine (whilst enjoying it responsibly, of course!). There's always something new to explore, whether it be a grape, a region or a producer.

If you've bought or been gifted this book, the chances are you are already a wine enthusiast looking to find out a little more. My advice is to start with what you already know you like and expand out from there. A fan of Argentinian Malbec? Flick through the book and find out which other regions specialise in Malbec grapes (I'll do this one for you – Cahors, page 72), then give that a try and see if you can taste how the different landscapes and climates have impacted on what's in the bottle. Love a Barolo but looking for something younger and slightly lighter in tannin? Try a Barbaresco.

If you're ever unsure or see something on a label or a wine menu that you don't understand, then get out your phone (or better yet, this book!) and look it up. If you happen upon a bottle of wine that you really love, take a picture of the label and use that as a jumping off point next time you order. My hope is that this book has given you the tools to be able to make more informed decisions based on your likes and dislikes, and maybe expand your horizons slightly. The single most important thing to remember is that wine is there to be enjoyed.

Salut!
Fred

Glossary

Acidity: Wines that are higher in acid will taste tart on the palate, whereas low-acidity wines are smoother and mellower. Wines with good acidity are crisp and refreshing – a desirable trait in white wines, especially.

Aeration: Exposing wine to oxygen to soften its edges and allow it to open up. *See also* Breathing.

Aging: Laying down wine to allow its structure to develop. Beneficial for complex wines that are high in tannins.

Alcohol: Produced through the fermentation of sugar and yeast. The ABV (alcohol by volume) percentage will be clearly marked on a wine label. Wines with higher alcohol levels can cause a slight burning sensation at the back of the throat.

Appellation: A legally defined area in which wines are produced. Appellations can be very large, covering whole regions, or as small as individual vineyards, and each is subject to its own specific rules around grape growing and wine production.

Astringency: The mouth-drying quality of wines that are high in tannins.

Blend: A wine that is made from the juices of more than one grape varietal.

Body: The heft or weight of a wine in the glass and mouth. Full-bodied wines will taste rich and full in your mouth, whereas lighter wines are thinner and often more refreshing.

Botrytis: Also known as Noble Rot, a mould that weakens the skin of grapes and accelerates the evaporation of water, resulting in grapes that are higher in residual sugars. Highly beneficial in the production of dessert wines.

Bouquet: The complex aromas that can be detected when sniffing a glass of wine. One of the strongest indicators of how a wine will taste.

Breathing: Allowing wine to sit, opened and often decanted, for a period of time before drinking, thus exposing the wine to oxygen and helping it to open up slightly.

Chaptalization: Adding sugar to wine during fermentation to increase the alcohol level and, in some cases, sweeten the wine.

Cork taint: The spoiled, musty taste and aroma detectable in wines that are described as 'corked'. Caused by the presence of the chemical compounds 2,4,6-Trichloroanisole (TCA) or 2,4,6-Tribromoanisole (TBA) which are by-products of wood production.

Cuvée: French word for 'blend', often associated with Champagne. A *cuvée* can be made up of different grape varietals and also different vintages of the same varietal.

Fermentation: The process of vinifying grape juice into wine with yeast and sugar.

Flor: The white layer of yeast that forms over the surface of fortified wines, particularly sherry, during fermentation. Protects the wine from exposure to oxygen during the fermentation process.

Lees: The dead yeast cells left over at the end of fermentation, sometimes visible at the bottom of a bottle of wine and referred to as sediment. Wines that are in contact with lees in the bottle for long periods can develop a nutty, bready flavour that can be desirable.

Mouthfeel: The texture of a wine in the mouth, from full-bodied and mouth-coating to thin and refreshing.

Must: Unfermented grape juice that includes the skins, stems and seeds from the grapes.

Oaked: Wines that have been stored in oak barrels after fermentation. Highly oaked wines take on the qualities and flavours of the wood, often presenting with rich, spicy flavours and notes of vanilla.

Oxidized: Wine that has been overexposed to oxygen and changed in structure as a result. Delicate, older wines can quickly deteriorate when exposed to air.

Phylloxera: Tiny insects that feast on the roots and leaves of grapevines with catastrophic results. See page 192.

Sommelier: A trained wine waiter in a restaurant.

Tannins: Bitter and astringent phenolic compounds that can be appealing when balanced with other qualities in fine wines. Found in the skins and stems of the grape, so wines made from grapes with thicker skins tend to be higher in tannins.

Terroir: The unique geographical, climatical and (sometimes) traditional make-up of a region that leaves its mark on a wine.

Vinification: Winemaking.

Vintage: The year in which a wine is produced.

Yield: The output of a vineyard in a single winemaking season.

Index